NAMASTEY BHARAT

NAMASTEY BHARAT

CHURNING THE SOFT POWER TREASURE OF INDIA

DR. PREETHI AMARESH

GenNext Publication

Published by

GenNext Publication
5, Ansari Road
Daryaganj, New Delhi-110002
Phone: 011-47034999, 9811692060
E-mail: gennextpublication@hotmail.com

Distribution Network
gyanbooks.com
India, USA, Canada, UK, Australia, France

ISBN: 978-93-5663-102-1
"An Imprint of Kalpaz Publication"
First Published, 2023

Printed at: Gyan Press, Delhi.

Namastey Bharat
Author: Dr. Preethi Amaresh

I dedicate this book to…

The New Bharat (India)…a Superpower in Making!

Contents

Abstract

This book takes the reader through India's journey in the arena of soft power from ancient times until the contemporary era. India as one of the oldest civilization has had its long path of journey from being called the "Golden Bird" to becoming one of the most important countries in the world today at the global podium.

Today, the importance of India has ascended due to the power shift in the global geopolitics as many scholars and experts talk about the rise of the "Asian century". This book is an in-depth study conducted on India's soft power, which includes predominant elements on soft power such as civil society, foreign policy, public diplomacy, cultural diplomacy and likewise a comparison with the soft power of China.

The book on the whole aims at revisiting the country's super-abundant sof† power, appreciating the several rich soft power aspects that Mystic India possesses. It also highlights the several gaps that require to be filled for the country to further work towards advancing its soft power in the 21st century to become a "soft power-superpower".

Acknowledgement

I am grateful and thankful to Mr. Amit Garg (Director), GYAN publication house (New Delhi) for providing me this wonderful opportunity to publish the book.

I am privileged, overwhelmed and content to complete this book, which was a compilation of my doctoral thesis. My Doctorate of International Relations (DIR) programme in Geneva School of Diplomacy, Switzerland would have been difficult without my family's great support and their persevering patience, encouragement helped me to lift up my confidence and complete the thesis successfully. I would like to thank my mother Shyla (a retired central government banker) and my sister Swetha (an engineer residing in Australia) for being my great support, who will always remain a motivational factor in my continued success. I would also like to express my gratitude to Mr. Amaresh, my late father and a former central government banker.

As part of my Doctoral journey I would like to thank my university Geneva School of Diplomacy who were very cooperative and supportive.

Furthermore, I would like to thank the following universities and institutions such as the National Institute of Advanced Studies (India), Moscow State Institute of International Relations (MGIMO, Russia), Russian International Affairs Council (RIAC), NIAS (University of Copenhagen) and South African Military Academy (Stellenbosch University) where, as a visiting doctoral scholar, my further research on soft power helped me in gaining additional inputs on the following topic. Furthermore, I would like to extend my gratitude to the Development Partnership Administration (Foreign Ministry of India, New Delhi) for inviting me and providing more insights about India's soft power.

Lastly, I would like to extend special thanks my husband Captain Sushanth (an Air India Pilot) for motivating me to successfully complete the research.

Quotes

"I do not like carving the world into segments; we are one world".

— Indira Gandhi

"A nation's strength ultimately consists in what it can do on its own, and not in what it can borrow from others."

— Indira Gandhi

A country's greatness lies in its undying ideals of love and sacrifice that inspire the mothers of the race.

— Sarojini Naidu

"The Indian way of life provides the vision of the natural and real way of life. We veil ourselves with unnatural masks. On the face of India are the tender expressions which carry the mark of the creator's hand".

— George Bernard Shaw

"India was the motherland of our race, and Sanskrit the mother of Europe's languages: she was the mother of our philosophy; mother of self-government and democracy".

— Will Durant

"There is no book in the world that is so thrilling, stirring and inspiring as the Upanishads".

— Max Muller

"We owe a lot to the Indians, who taught us how to count without which no worthwhile scientific discovery could have been made".

— Albert Einstein

"In the name of democracy let us all unite and fight for a new India"

— Indian National Congress

"My nationalism is as broad as my Swadeshi, I want India's rise so that the whole world may benefit".

— Mahatma Gandhi

"India is a country in which every great religion finds a home"

— Annie Besant

"Many of the advances in the sciences that we consider today to have been made in Europe were in fact made in India centuries ago."

— Grant Duff, British Historian

"India is the cradle of the human race, the birthplace of human speech, the mother of history, the grandmother of legend and the great grand mother of tradition. Our most valuable and most constructive materials in the history of man are treasured up in India only".

— Mark Twain

"Culture is the widening of the mind and of the spirit".

— Jawaharlal Nehru

"India is an old country but a young nation... I am young nation...I am young and I too have a dream, I dream of India strong, Independent, self-reliant and in the front rank of the nations of the world, in the service of mankind".

— Rajiv Gandhi

"If India wants to be a great nation, we must have courage to trust. This is my sincere belief".

— Dhirubhai Ambani

"I dream of an India that is prosperous, strong and caring. An India, that regains a place of honor in the comity of great nations."

— Atal Bihari Vajpayee

"This country has not been made by politicians, kings or governments. It has been made by saints, farmers, laborers and the people".

— Narendra Modi

"We will be remembered only if we give to our younger generation a prosperous and safe India, resulting out of economic prosperity coupled with civilizational heritage".

— APJ Abdul Kalam

"The young people of India will build a strong and powerful nation, a nation that is politically mature and economically strong, a nation whose people enjoy both a high quality of life as well as justice".

— Pranab Mukherjee

"If there is one place on the face of this earth where all the dreams of living men have found from the very earliest days when man began the dream of existence, it is India".

— Romain Rolland

"I am proud of my country. But we need to unite to make a unified India, free of communalism and casteism. We need to build India into a land of equal opportunity for all. We can be a truly great nation if we set our sights high and deliver to the people the fruits of continued growth, prosperity and equal opportunity".

— Ratan Tata

"A nation's culture resides in the hearts and in the soul of its people."

— Mahatma Gandhi

"It is true that even across the Himalayan barrier India has sent to the west, such gifts as grammar and logic, philosophy and fables, hypnotism and chess, and above all numerals and the decimal system".

— Will Durant

"India conquered and dominated China culturally for 20 centuries without ever having to send a single soldier across her border".

— Hu Shih

"After the conversations about Indian philosophy, some of the ideas of Quantum Physics that had seemed crazy suddenly made much more sense".

— W. Heisenberg

"There are some parts of the world that, once visited, get into your heart and won't go. For me, India is such a place".

— Keith Bellows

Acronyms

APF	Akshaya Patra Foundation
AI	Artificial Intelligence
AIIB	Asian Infrastructure Investment Bank
AIEI	Association of Indian Engineering Industry
ASSOCHAM	Associated Chambers of Commerce and Industry of India
AAGC	Asia-Africa Growth Corridor
ASEAN	Association of Southeast Asian Nations
AIIB	Asian Infrastructure Investment Bank
BCIM	Bangladesh, China, India and Myanmar Economic Corridor
BRI	Belt and Road Initiative
BIMSTEC	Bay of Bengal Initiative for Multi-Sectoral Technical and Economic Cooperation
BRICS	Brazil, Russia, India, China and South Africa
BBC	British Broadcasting Corporation
CWG	Commonwealth Games
CLAWS	Centre for Land Warfare Studies
CIs	Confucius Institutes
CON	Commonwealth of Nations
CEEW	Council On Energy, Environment and Water
CDR	Centre for Dialogue and Reconciliation
CDRI	Coalition for Disaster Resilient Infrastructure
CICA	Confidence Building Measures in Asia
CSOs	Civil Society Organizations
COVID	Corona Virus Disease

CCP	Chinese Communist Party
CMs	Chief Ministers
CD	Cultural diplomacy
CCTV	China Central Television
CII	Confederation of Indian Industry
DD	Digital diplomacy
DPA	Development Partnership Administration
DPSP	Fundamental Rights and Directive Principles of State Policy
DONER	Development of the North Eastern Region
ECOWAS	Economic Community of West African States
EU	European Union
ICJ	International Court of Justice
ICLU	Indian Civil Liberties union
ICS	Indian Cultural Services
IR	International relations
IT	Information technology
IPE	International political economy
IMF	International Monetary Fund
IFIs	International financial institutions
FIDC	Forum for Indian Development Cooperation
FICCI	Federation of Indian chambers of commerce and Industry
FFP	Feminist Foreign Policy
FCRA	Foreign Currency Regulation Act
FTAs	Free trade agreements
FDI	Foreign Direct Investment
GOI	Government of India
GDP	Gross Domestic Product
G-4	Group-4
G-20	Group-20
INGOs	International Nongovernmental Organizations

ICWA	Indian Council of World Affairs
IDSA	Institute for Defence Studies and Analyses
IOs	International Organizations
INC	Indian National Congress
ICLU	Indian Civil Liberties union
ICT	Information and communications technology
ICCR	Indian Council for Cultural Relations
IOR	Indian Ocean Region
J&K	Jammu and Kashmir
KIP	Know India Programme
LPG	Liberalization, Privatization and Globalization
LAC	Line of Actual Control
MAD	Make A Difference
MNCs	Multinational Companies
MGNREGA	Mahatma Gandhi Rural Employment Guarantee Act
MHRD	Ministry Human Resources and Development
MEA	Ministry of External Affairs
NEC	North Eastern Council
NPT	Nuclear Non-Proliferation Treaty
NAC	National Advisory Council
NEST	New Emerging and Strategic Technologies
NGOs	Non-governmental organizations
NAM	Non Alignment Movement
NDB	New Development Bank
NSC	New Security Concept
NKC	National Knowledge Commission
NDA	National Democratic Alliance
NHGs	Neighborhood Groups
NER	Northeast region
NRLM	National Rural Livelihoods Mission

NREGA	National Rural Employment Guarantee
NRIs	Non Resident Indians
ORF	Observer Research Foundation
OIA	Overseas Indian Affairs
OPEC	Organization of the Petroleum Exporting Countries
PD	Public diplomacy
PDS	Public distribution system
PM-CARES	Prime Minister's Citizen Assistance and Relief in Emergency Situations
PACS	Poorest Areas Civil Society
PMO	Prime Minister's Office
PETA	People for the Ethical Treatment of Animals
PKO	Peacekeeping operations
PIL	Public Interest Litigation
PM	Prime minister
PIOs	Persons of Indian origins
PRC	Peoples Republic of China
P-5	Permanent Five
RTE	Right to Education
RTI	Right To Information
RSS	Rashtriya Swayamsevak Sangh
R&D	Research and Development
SCO	Shanghai Cooperation Organization
SAARC	South Asian Association for Regional Cooperation
SHGs	Self Help Groups
SCS	South China Sea
SCIO	State Council Information Office of China
TFI	Teach for India
TRP	Target rating point
UNESCO	United Nations Educational, Scientific and Cultural Organization

UNGA	United Nations General Assembly
UNSC	United Nations Security Council
UTs	Union Territories
UPA	United Progressive Government
UNFPA	United Nations Population Fund
U.N	United Nations
U.K	United Kingdom
U.S	United States
UNCRC	United Nations Convention on the Rights of the Child
UDHR	Universal Declaration of Human Rights
VIF	Vivekananda International Foundation
VJAS	Vidarbha Jan Andolan Samiti
WHO	World Health Organization
WTO	World Trade Organization
UNCTAD	United Nations Conference on Trade and Development
WION	World Is One News
WEF	World Economic Forum
XPD	External Publicity and Public Diplomacy

Chapter One

Prologue: India - The Soft Power Treasure of the world

1.1 India's Soft Power: Ancient to Modern India

The promise of India lies in its centuries old culture, large and young population, size and potential of the economy. The geography and forces of nature have played an important role in the evolution of Indian history. India as a nation is opulently enriched with unique flora and fauna, which is an active cultural-anthropological gallery. The subcontinent has seen a great deal of migration and churn. People, ideas and trade have moved in different directions at different points of time and for different reasons. India, as an identity being the oldest civilization (Indus valley), has influenced the west since time primeval and has further showcased itself as a novel civilization by embracing a clearly expressed and tolerant use of building its civilization[1]. Indus valley civilization, being the most classical and the oldest civilization in the world is a marvelous example of India's soft power.

India is an enlightened nation with a vibrant cultural inheritance and has evermore maintained an engaging traditional society, including finding its feet to the global popular culture besides consisting of a bewildering mix of castes, tribes, and languages groups. The country's rich civilization and its past achievements are a source of immense pride, justification for a sense of superiority and progressing towards a great future. The traditional and age-old, description of the Hindu faith as an understanding and pluralistic faith has served India to define itself as a non-violent and tolerant society. India as a nation has had plenty more to contribute in courses of its connections with other parts of the world. The country has had a vibrant and traditional history that has given rise to several academicians, intellectuals and scholars that have committed to the conception of distinct followings of knowledge, a India is an enlightened nation with a vibrant cultural inheritance and has evermore maintained an engaging traditional society, including finding its feet to the global popular culture besides consisting of a bewildering mix of castes, tribes, and languages groups. The country's rich civilization and its past achievements are a source of immense pride, justification for a sense of superiority and progressing towards a great future. The traditional and age-old, description of the Hindu faith as an understanding and pluralistic faith has served India to define itself as a non-violent and tolerant society. India as a nation has had plenty more to contribute in courses of its connections with other parts of the world. The country has had a vibrant and traditional history that has given rise to several academicians, intellectuals and scholars that have committed to the conception of distinct followings of knowledge, a pearl of wisdom that has travelled and set themselves far exceeding its frontiers. The country likewise has had an abundance of expertise in the field of economics, government, migration, traditional knowledge, higher learning, law and order.

India's broad soft power assets furthermore extend to the disciplines of science where in the ancient India many great scientists and intellectuals have committed extensively to astronomy, science and mathematics. Similarly, the ancient universities of India such as the Nalanda etc. were the most prominent centers of cultural synergy and soft power, which drew a great number of scholars and learners from different parts of the world. Later, the scholars and academicians from such great universities carried with them, the culture of India to other countries along with their knowledge and faith. On the whole, India had an extraordinary economic, intellectual and cultural influence throughout the ancient world. Excelling the charts of India's soft power is its spirituality or holiness. Spirituality in India has been nourished and acknowledged to further flourish and grow. This has given birth to major religions of the world such as Hinduism, Jainism, Buddhism, and Sikhism. India is therefore dedicated to having all the notable faiths of the globe such as Hinduism, Jainism, Buddhism, and Sikhism that arose in India and Islam, Judaism, Christianity and Zoroastrianism that came from outside. India is also home to thousands of languages and several religious monuments. India's global representation is thus rooted in the idea of 'unity in diversity', contemplative of the wide collection of cultures and civilizations that remains to attract many across the world. Likewise, in ancient India, the country was known as the land of knowledge, golden bird, precious stones, spices, merchants and navigators[2].

In the subsequent years, medieval India gave way to the spread of Bhakti movement and Sufism, which were acknowledged for their peaceful, universal notions and customs. Indian philosopher Swami Vivekananda precisely reflected in the message of global cultural space along with unity and peace from India at the 'World Conference of Religions' held in Chicago. Swami Vivekananda further asserted, "For our motherland, a connection of the two great systems, Hinduism and Islam—Vedanta Brain and Islam Body—is the only hope" (Mehta, 2012)[3]. However, the disintegration of the Mughal Empire left the country in chaos during the 18th century. In the 19th century, there were efforts by Indian reformers to harmonize religion with a rationalist picture of the world. Prominent among the reformers were Raja Ram Mohan Roy, Ishwar Chandra Vidyasagar and Debendranath Tagore. Emphasizing modernity, Roy sought to synthesize scientific thought with Indian culture and religion. Rather than attempting to turn back the clock to restore a golden age of former glory, he represented the thinking that characterizes modernizing viewpoint in the Indian civil society. The "Bengal Renaissance" further began with questioning of religious tradition and involved contemporary science, literature, history and western education.

Furthermore, empires came and went but social structures such as caste and community remained. The British in India inherited this legacy and continued the practice. They segregated the Indian society along the community lines and exacerbated the differences between various religious communities. Nevertheless, the British's legacy in India is usually analyzed from an economic perspective. Britain overpowered India through looting, expropriation, and outright theft [4]. Will Durant, an American scholar called Britain's colonial conquest of India "the greatest crime in all history[5]." Indian nationalist, Dadabhai Naoroji further referred to the British conquest of India as "Drain of wealth" (economic exploitation and flow of wealth to Britain). The India that the British dominated was not primitive but the "glittering jewel" of the medieval world[6]. Angus Maddison, a British economic historian has heralded that, at the beginning of the 18th century, India's share of the international economy was 23 per cent, which is as huge as all of Europe put together[7]. Also, when the Mughal emperor Aurangzeb's treasury collected 100 million pounds in tax revenues alone, it was 27 per cent in 1700[8]. But, by the time the British exited India, the economy plunged to just over 3 per cent[9]. Thereafter, India had been therefore reduced from a land of merchants or traders, artisans and warriors working in prosperous and intricate commercial networks into an agricultural community of peasants and moneylenders[10].

By the 18th century, the country was clearly far behind Europe and it was the change in cultural attitude towards innovation and the outside world that led to technological stagnation and eventually to economic and civilizational decline. Furthermore, the Indian national movement was a political struggle for independence and a movement for societal change and Mahatma Gandhi (father of the nation) further championed gradual reform from within the society. Recovering from colonial rule, India sought to rebuild a sense of national pride by drawing on its glorious past. The Indian national movement that led to end of colonial rule was built on India's great prospects.

India thus has an optimistic vision of relatively pluralistic government, non-violent, and liberal with a non-threatening global leadership. Distinguished personages like Gandhi, Rabindranath Tagore and Films, literature, music, yoga, dance, software industry, Ayurveda etc., produce an extraordinary array of soft power assets that portray the attractiveness of India to the foreign audience. In India, the power of appeal and charm also stems from chief institutional arrangements of secularism, democracy, federalism, and India's three-language formula, which have descended from the nation's comprehensive civilization regardless of profound stratified matters emanating from corruption and the caste system. However, the country's democracy has maintained itself.

The importance of respect, harmony and fraternity are the essences that Indians are recognized for, with Ashoka, Buddha and Mahatma Gandhi standing as principal representatives. The Indian intellectuals and freedom warriors such as Bal Gangadhar Tilak, Mahatma Gandhi, Swami Vivekananda, Sri Aurobindo, Jawaharlal Nehru, Sardar Patel and Lal Bahadur Shastri oftentimes highlighted on the union of distinct cultures and values for enhancing the status of India. Nehru's concept "unity in diversity" further conceptualizes this synthetic character of India's soft power. The 'Incredible India' tourism campaign likewise offered an indispensable role in advancing 'Brand India', being a catchphrase to describe the campaign started by India to draw interest and represent the country as a productive purpose for investment.

Besides Indian being the world's largest democracy, its traditional soft power elements such as spiritualism, yoga, Ayurveda, Sanskrit language, movies and television, classical and popular dance forms and music, cuisines, principles of non-violence, democratic institutions, plural society, the role of Civil Society Organizations (CSOs) have all attracted people across the world. Moreover, 'Culture' as the creation of soft power diplomacy, known as the significant instrument of India's foreign policy has enhanced ties amongst people overseas, which has helped India to magnify its position in regional and bilateral ties, regardless of the consequences for its ample power aspirations. Also, the United Nations General Assembly (UNGA) in 2014 announced the 21st of June to be commemorated as "International Yoga Day", which was started by India and is viewed as an expression of the country's soft power. "Buddhism" likewise is considered to be an essential bridge between India and South East Asia, South Asia and East Asia. The Indian space programs, Jaipur literature festival (largest literary event in Asia), and India art summit have additionally enriched the country's soft power.

Similarly, Indian spiritual leaders such as Swami Vivekananda, Aurobindo and lately Sri Ravishankar and Sadhguru have tremendous followings globally. In the contemporary era, through the vision of Vasudhaiva Kutumbhkam (the whole world is a family) and incredible soft power components, in the 21st century, India could effortlessly be a model globally. The impression of Indian civilization and culture is the most powerful throughout the world and soft power has become a piece of crucial equipment in also determining India's foreign policy and strategic decisions. The soft power of India has likewise increased its capability to connect, strengthen the connections and to fix the fractures shaped by the country's history and politics. India's civilization is her contribution to the world and it reflects the evolution of the country's history, how India greatly immersed other cultures but never relinquished its civilization and culture. The international image of India has thus been rooted in the perception of 'unity in diversity', contemplative of the extensive checkerboard of art and cultures that extends to draw many across the world. India has risen to obtain an edge over others in terms of soft power. Since from more than a decade, India has elevated its indispensable resources in public diplomacy (PD), by applying traditional and innovative channels to create and anchorage its soft power.

India has further proclaimed springing ideologies of individualism, liberality, secularism and universalism. Considering that hard power cannot be exercised exceeding a frontier or territory, it is soft power that can boost the image of India and create a niche for the country in the modern global system. Modern India's essential purposes and traditions moreover carry glorious hope for accomplishing multi-ethnic communities, notably in the emerging world.

Similarly, International organizations (IOs) and transnational partnerships perform a prominent role in their augmentation of soft power. The flow of foreign policy within IOs is an extra channel through which nations manifest patience and perseverance apt to others where soft power is displayed. As an advocate of co-operation between sovereign between sovereign nations, India has been member of several major IOs such as the United Nations (U.N), World Health Organization (WHO), etc. and also regional organizations such as Shanghai Cooperation Organization (SCO), Association of Southeast Asian Nations (ASEAN), Brazil, Russia, India, China and South Africa (BRICS), South Asian Association for Regional Cooperation (SAARC), Bay of Bengal Initiative for Multi-Sectoral Technical and Economic Cooperation (BIMSTEC) etc. Importantly, India was one of the founding members of the U.N in 1945, even before independence and played a critical role throughout the era of decolonization. Similarly, India has been a robust proponent of inter-cultural and inter-civilizational dialogue as one of the most revered members of The United Nations Educational, Scientific and Cultural Organization (UNESCO).

India further sought a greater voice for itself and other developing nations in the Bretton woods system while also helping to lay the foundations of new institutions like the BRICS bank and Asian Infrastructure Investment Bank (AIIB) where the developing world might have a greater say. Currently, India along with Brazil, Germany and Japan is part of the group of four nations (G4) that see themselves as worthy of permanent membership for the expansion of the United Nations Security Council (UNSC). In the area of foreign policy, India during cold war adopted a policy of non-alignment movement (NAM) to build relations with developing nations and the western countries. India's leaders sought to advance the nation's interest by securing technology and modern techniques from communist and capitalist countries. At the end of the cold war, India's economic liberalization, sustained democracy, its embrace of technology, its culturally diverse society led to resurrection of the promise of India. Post-Cold War and India's 1991 Liberalization, Privatization and Globalization (LPG) reforms, there was opening up of economies of India. Today, India supports multilateralism but it also seeks to reform global agencies which it feels are influenced heavily by the world's major powers.

While humanitarian associations generally and indirectly mediate soft power, diplomatic aid additionally provides an added immediate passage to soft power. "Diplomacy" is indeed a tool for heightening soft power. So, if India seeks to become a great power it needs to spend more money on enhancing its diplomatic outreach globally and establishing think tanks in the country that can act as a bridge between state and civil society apart from spending on defence. Lately, a reinvigorated focus on the indispensable augmentation of civil society to a flexible international system besides business and government has increased. The power and the progression of civil society continue to thrive which requires to be equipped to build trust and facilitate progress across sectors. Scholars and specialists from industry, state and IOs have further penned the significance of the functions that civil society performs as a segment of the more comprehensive governance system. Also, due to cross-border impediments, Indian CSOs have become fundamental stakeholders in defining international norms. Partha Chatterjee has explained India civil society as a middle-class sphere confined to a reasonably small section of citizens, prominently the middle classes who articulate the expression of rights[11]. The government of India (GOI) consequently has a pivotal part to perform in strengthening civil society and public rendezvous on foreign policy and increasing partnership matters, apart from also maintaining any interest that these actors begin in the following field. Civil society is the ultimate symbol of a place of struggle among distinctive kinds of associations and engagements. The country needs to therefore exhibit the determined role of civil society in the construction of a brand-new India.

Moving further in the context of the diaspora, India is a distinguished and likely reservoir of remarkable notions and values that are broadly embraced, exemplified and functioned by the Indian diaspora in various parts globally. The term, Indian Diaspora has been used to address the population who have migrated from the territories that are present within the borders of India. There are an estimated 17.5 million Indian Diasporas that include PIOs (Persons of Indian origins) and NRIs (Non-resident Indians)[12]. Soft power is not solely confined to the power and prospects of the diaspora or fostering the connections with the diaspora. However, it can help promote a state to influence globally by promoting diaspora as cultural envoys, while creating commercial profits from remittances and ventures of the diaspora. Today, notably, several Indian diaspora have occupied prominent positions across the world in various professional fields like politics, diplomacy, technology, medicine, art, literature etc. making India proud.

A vibrant and robust economy is oftentimes not sufficient for nations to sustain their aspirations. In this information era with free mobility of people, insights, capital, thoughts weigh stronger than ever. That is when soft power becomes necessary. Presently, the Ministry of External Affairs (MEA) to project India's soft power globally and across world capitals has ventured on a program to construct diplomatic missions and cultural centers through India's myriad types of architecture. GOI policies like the 'Act East Policy, 'Neighborhood First Policy', 'Connect Central Asia Policy' and lately 'Digital Diplomacy' and 'Para-Diplomacy' absolutely are considered to be robust soft power elements. Today, India's aspirations can be treated as an international leader of world governance, being regarded as an international developing economy and the most comprehensive democracy globally. In directing the country towards a brand new India, interestingly, India has also greatly created a huge impact in Switzerland that sprang up a brand-India campaign at the yearly conference of the World Economic Forum (WEF) in 2006, at Davos, Switzerland[13]. After the Davos conference, The New York Times penned the following caption "India Everywhere in the Alps"[14]. India's nation branding initiatives such as the "Incredible India campaign", "Make In India", "Digital India", "Start-Up India", "Skill India", "Project Mausam" and implying to the country's history, culture and tradition in addresses or talks are some soft power instruments that carry the country's ambitious identification and potential to the world. Similarly, the 'Raisina dialogue', a multilateral conference hosted by Observer Research Foundation (ORF) and MEA aim to search possibilities and opportunities for the Asian synthesis and its integration with the larger world[15]. The dialogue also highlighted that for such an amalgamation India requires to perform a crucial role that will help the country to play a vital role in the Indian Ocean Region (IOR) and also support in building a stable regional and world order.

India has also done remarkably well in Information technology (IT) and software. In this context, Indian Prime minister (PM) Modi asserted that "India's journey has progressed from snake charmers to mouse charmers!" appending, "the youth of the country has its finger on the mouse of computers and is changing the world"[16]. "Snake charmers" here represents a connection to the country's spiritualism, superstitions, mysticism, poverty and backwardness[17]. "Mouse (Computer) charmers" displays to the mounting profile of India as an IT power, rising middle class, its economic growth, human resource and thriving ambitions (The Economic Times, 2013)[18]. Today, diplomacy in India has further hailed technological changes as various ministries; diplomats and political leaders have been in favor of social media to practice diplomacy. Embassies, consulates, foreign ministries, diplomats have practiced Digital diplomacy (DD) including the non-state actors like human rights groups and civil society.

The post-COVID (Corona Virus Disease) world order is susceptible to the rise of middle powers such as India and the country through its extensive foreign policy approach should project itself as an accountable and reliable global stakeholder. The value of multilateralism is necessary to preserve the world order post-COVID and India being a middle power should uniquely be positioned to help resuscitate multilateralism and take charge of the leadership. Importantly, PD of the 19th century will not be relevant today. Therefore, in addition to diplomats, countries must engage other non-state actors like think tanks and practitioners, to formulate plans. By 2024, India will be the most popular country and by 2028 it is expected to become world's third largest economy[19]. Nonetheless, India could be a world leader in not just economic terms but also as a vibrant, free and dynamic country. As per Yashwant Sinha, the former Indian foreign minister, 'India lives in every century of time". Nevertheless, in the mounting multipolar global order, India needs to enhance its position further.

The contemporary world is based on the puzzle of international relations (IR). After deleterious world wars, society as a whole is experiencing a rendezvous with numerous global situations. India's capacity to construct and consistently maintain a democratic political system has further made the country a natural partner for the western democracies. Having a fairly non-threatening and neutral image, the soft power of India has rare features in comparison to the outstanding countries of the emerging multipolar world like China, the U.S., Japan and Russia [20]. Also, India and China are considered to be the only contemporary great powers that have maintained a predominantly successive culture for several millennia[21]. In the 21st century, the influence of soft power of India at the global platform has been a great passageway before the word was adopted universally with India being known as the melting pot of cultures, beliefs and languages. Being one of the two oldest continuous civilizations in the world, India could certainly be a global power but the country has to fill certain gaps and challenges to be one. India's promise cannot be realized without acknowledging its failings.

India's soft power resources could be subsequently promoted and skillfully used to promote its foreign policy interests if the GOI inconspicuously generates infrastructural backing for soft undertakings and refrains from meddling in the social and cultural lives of its people. Maria Wirth, a German writer remarked that 'India has the deepest philosophy still expressed in a vibrant religion, a huge body of literature, dance, music, amazing art, architecture, appetizing cuisine and yet Indians are in denial mode and wake up only when foreigners treasure India[22]'. However, India seems reluctant and bewildered in developing the right blend of soft and hard power apart from realizing its magnificent soft power resources. India comprehends that it wants to be a great power because it is its right to be, however, India's march towards its great power status is not likely to be as smooth as it sounds. Even as the promise of a rising India keeps resurfacing, it is held back by inadequate modernization. Indians believe in the greatness of India based on its rich past but the question is when and how will the country manifest itself on the world stage.

Notes

1. Varma, A. (2021) *India, the oldest civilization, is finally being able to establish its identity*.

   Available at: https://timesofindia.indiatimes.com/blogs/no-free-lunch/india-The-oldest-civilization-is-finally-being-able-to-establish-its-identity/ (Accessed: 21 June 2022)
2. Bhattacharya.S, Sahasrabuddhe.V, Mukherjee. A, Sachdev.B.K. (2021), "An analytic interpretation on the Importance of India's soft power in international cultural diplomacy over the centuries", *World Journal of Advanced Research and Reviews*, 2021, 12(03), 131–136, DOI: 10.30574/wjarr.2021.12.3.0995
3. Mehta.P.B (2012*), What Vivekananda valued, The Indian Express*. Available at: https://indianexpress.com/article/opinion/columns/what-vivekananda-valued/ (Accessed: 14 October 2020)
4. Tharoor. S (2017), *The Price of Empire, Project Syndicate*. Available at: https://www.project-Syndicate.org/commentary/uk-india-relations-colonization-by-shashi-tharoor-2017-02 (Accessed: 4 June 2020)
5. *Ibid.*
6. Tharoor.S (2016) *An Era of Darkness: The British Empire in India*. India: Aleph publication.
7. *Ibid.*
8. *Ibid.*
9. *Ibid.*
10. *Ibid.*
11. Bhattacharyya. H (2021) Partha Chatterjee's concepts of civil society and 'uncivil' political Society: Is the distinction valid? *Journal of Civil Society*, 17:1, 18-33, DOI: 10.1080/17448689.2021.1886759
12. PTI. (2019) *At 17.5 million, Indian diaspora largest in the world: UN report*. Available at:

    https://www.thehindu.com/news/international/at-175-million-indian-diaspora-largest-in-the-world-un-report/article30105882.ece (Accessed: January 15 2020)
13. Landler, M. (2006) *India Everywhere' in the Alps*, Available at:

    https://www.nytimes.com/2006/01/26/business/worldbusiness/india-everywhere-in-the-alps.html (Accessed: 6 November 2019)
14. Ibid
15. Chaudhury. D. R (2022) *Raisina Dialogue will focus on six pillars, including Indo-Pacific and high Tech.* Available at: https://economictimes.indiatimes.com/news/india/raisina-dialogue-Will-focus-on-six-pillars-including-indo-pacific-and-high-tech/articleshow/91037208.cms (Accessed: 6 June 2022)

16. PTI. (2013) *10 punch lines from Narendra Modi's speech at SRCC*. Available at: https://economictimes.indiatimes.com/people/10-punch-lines-from-narendra-modis-speech-at- srcc/slideshow/18370143.cms (Accessed: 9 November 2019)

17. *Ibid.*

18. *Ibid.*

19. PTI. (2013) *India to be world's 3rd largest economy by 2028 after China, US*. Available at:

    https://economictimes.indiatimes.com/news/economy/indicators/india-to-be-worlds-3rd-Largest-economy-by-2028-after-china-us/articleshow/28006654.cms? from=mdr (Accessed: 3 December 2019)

20. Pethiyagoda, K (2014) *India's Soft Power Advantage*. Available at:

    https://thediplomat.com/2014/09/indias-soft-power-advantage/ (Accessed 3 January 2020)

21. *Ibid.*

22. Tharoor. S (2012) *Pax Indica: India and the world of the 21st Century*. New Delhi: Penguin India.

Chapter Two

Soft power spell-working in Indian foreign policy

2.1 Introduction to Foreign Policy

The notion of foreign policy dates back to primordial periods where foreign relations were conducted verbally with little archaeological evidence[1]. Foreign policy is conceived through high-level decision-making by the administration of the country and is driven and constructed by a mixture of characteristics such as political principles, geography, culture and diplomacy, history of the nation, domestic and socio-economic necessities, internal and external trade, peace accords, long-term debts and import of technology[2]. The foreign policy of a nation is implemented keeping in mind the condition in different regions internationally as well. In the present century foreign policy is comparable to establishments like national interests, embassies, international relations and bureaucratic policies. Change and continuity are components of all foreign policies[3]. The foreign policy of a nation echoes continuity because it is established on the long-term state interests of the country besides reflecting the foresight and the idea of the foreign policymakers[4]. Besides, change is likewise an essential part of all foreign policies, which is vital because the background, both external and internal is frequently at fluctuation. Indian foreign policy in this context is no exception to this rule[5].

This chapter begins with Indian foreign policy and its development post-Independence and later advances towards contemporary soft power concepts of Indian foreign policy such as role of private sector, IOs etc., Para-diplomacy, PD, DD and CD in India.

2.2. Indian Foreign Policy: Important Developments Since Independence

Literature on Indian foreign policy presents a spectrum of approaches to the study of the subject. The study of Indian foreign policy has been dominated by literature on India's ties with China, Pakistan and the U.S. India was Britain's most important overseas possession, the "jewel" in the crown until the 19th century. However, since the country attained its freedom from Britain, it has developed institutions and strategies to foster a robust foreign policy even as core ideas and values from the country's history persist to inform India's foreign policy objectives[6]. Post-independence, Nehru quickly adopted a soft power strategy to foreign policy by focusing on establishing a distinct voice for post-colonial developing nations. His personal sense of moral import in PD and his preferred use of soft power over hard power molded the nature of the country's early foreign policy[7]. In the 1950s and 1960s, India put forth a foreign policy based on soft power through NAM, highlighting development, self-determination and partnerships[8]. Even post the 1962 India-China war India stayed the path by highlighting on 'mildly armed NAM' desiring that patient commitment to soft power might bear fruit.[9]. During the cold war years, India's IR oscillated between a somewhat idealist posture often associated with Nehru and realism favored by his daughter Indira Gandhi. Nehru saw the country's independence as part of a broader Asian resurgence where according to him foreign policy was a tool of making India's presence felt global.

Nehru saw the country's independence as part of a broader Asian resurgence where according to him foreign policy was a tool of making India's presence felt global[10]. Nehru and his successors acknowledged that India was a great nation and would produce leaders who would serve wisely where the position of global teacher and leader is positively valued[11]. Nehru resisted playing the position of Chakravarti (the classical Hindu leader) even as he filled it[12]. Mahatma Gandhi furthermore impacted the Nehruvian core directly via the Gandhi Nehru affinity and indirectly via the influence of the Mahatma on Indian thought at large[13]. Nehru stated that Indian foreign policy is leveled in the ancient Indian tradition and culture and opposed to western imperialism that could be outlined back to the ancient worldview of Indian perspective[14]. For Nehru, India was one of the two prominent Asian civilizations, which would exemplify the elevation of the continent[15]. In the 20th century, Nehru is considered one of the influencing statesmen besides being a critic of U.S imperialism, colonial exploitation and racial discrimination. The policy of NAM put forth by Nehru, symbolized the roots of the long Indian struggle for freedom. Through 17 long years of Prime Ministership, he structured the foreign policy of India at the cost of his principles. As the successor state to the British, Nehru's India included several regional policies such as the first three bilateral treaties that he signed with Nepal, Bhutan and Sikkim, shows his realism[16]. The policy of

NAM founded on the five principles of "Panchasheel", directed the global conduct. However, Panchasheel hit a setback during the India-China war in 1962.

According to strategist Subramanyan, while Nehruvian NAM was a grand strategy, the Indians did not consider the strategic consequences of NAM because India after 1947 saw itself as a non-expansionist and status quo-oriented power[17]. In his power as the PM, he attempted to blend the noblest segments of the east and the west[18]. He also maintained proximal ties with the British Commonwealth of Nations (CON) by promoting India as a member. But some see as Nehru's efforts to save the world from itself through NAM and disarmament, viewing as his neglect of Indian interests closer to home[19]. While others suggest that his diplomacy was wholly disconnected from any conception of national interest[20]. Nonetheless, Nehru's approach to foreign policy was both misguided and sincere[21]. Some also suggest that he took office as an idealist but had to adapt to realist posture later. For instance, Nehru quietly and deliberately laid the foundation for India's emergence as a nuclear power even as he called for nuclear disarmament[22]. He was also greatly interested in the U.N and believed that a robust U.N would serve important Indian interests. Nehru's successors have oftentimes been inspired by his diplomacy, and the themes he evoked as PM became integral in the discussion of Indian foreign policy[23]. Nehru's significant contribution was to state building as he adopted and nurtured the institutions that the British has put in place for almost a century[24].

Later, Shastri as the PM continued to follow the NAM besides developing close ties with the Soviet Union and shifting focus on the immediate neighborhood within South Asia. However, his tenure was short and he passed away following the Tashkent agreement. When Indira Gandhi, Nehru's daughter succeeded as the Indian PM ruling India for, the world was bipolar and she took charge when the country faced a rough external environment and occupied a fairly low standing in the global ranking of states. She acted as the PM from 1966 to 1977 and again from 1980 until her assassination in 1984, making her the second longest-serving Indian PM after her father Nehru. There was hegemony in South Asia as she is credited to have put forth the "Indira doctrine". As a military commander, she was immeasurably outstanding and superior. For example, her decisiveness during the 1971 war was in remarkable contrast to Nehru's indecisive attitude towards the Chinese[25]. This was brought to an end by signing the Shimla Agreement. Realists sometimes overestimate the role of tangible power and underestimate the importance of ideas, institutions and other attributes of soft power in IR[26]. In this context, Indira Gandhi having asserted military might like in the defeat Pakistan and economic strength to suppress Nepal, made no attempt to construct an institutional structure around the geographic, cultural, economic and historical aspects interlacing together the independent political entities living in South Asia[27]. During her tenure, developing nations such as India continued to look to developed nations and multilateral institutions for their needs. Although a pro-Soviet shift had established during the Nehru period in the practice of NAM, the Indo-Soviet Treaty of Peace and Friendship of 1971 signed during the Indira Gandhi era was the outcome of global circumstances and the transition of Indo-Soviet ties[28]. It also created a promising idea for the Soviet Union in Indian decision-makers and added to the association, particularly in the security domain. She will also be remembered by the nation for her determination to take nation on the path of a major power through the 1974 nuclear test exhibiting realism. But, sectarian violence and insurgencies within the country brought instability to a successful foreign policy and accumulation of power. India furthermore continued to be perceived as a 'soft state' under her emergency rule. However, Indira Gandhi was goal-oriented, pragmatic, flexible and non-ideological in her foreign policy, qualifying her as a realist[29]. The Indira doctrine embodied a formidable, uncompromising attitude towards neighbors both large and small[30]. Also, as per the book "Indira: India's most powerful Prime Minister" written by Sagarika Ghose, to this day, Indira Gandhi is still considered to be the most powerful PM of India. As for the 3 Cs (Character, Competence, and Charisma), Indira Gandhi was highly charismatic[31].

The nascent shift in foreign policy under Rajiv Gandhi, Indira Gandhi's son emanated from a confluence of external and internal elements[32]. He recognized the significance of foreign policy in advancing his domestic pursuits. In his first speeches in the office, Gandhi articulated his will to 'build India of the 21st century[33]. At the crux of his vision of modernization was the necessity to adopt high technology to alter the Indian society and economy[34]. China visit highlighted a critical aspect of his foreign policy and he was readied to make strategic stirs to settle in shielding Indian interests, while simultaneously examining diplomatic alternatives to resolve problems[35]. However, his biggest failure was in his handling of the Sri Lankan crisis[36]. He advanced to recast India's relations with China and the U.S. Although no great breakthroughs were attained, his engagement with them set the tone and pattern for the course and approach of all successive governments[37].

PV Narasimha Rao who succeeded Gandhi was one of the ablest leaders and was the foremost PM of India in the post-cold war period and the first

PM outside of the Nehru family to conclude a complete term in office[38]. His government redesigned Indian foreign policy to adapt to the new international setting[39]. FDI grew immensely and for the first time following its Independence, India was regarded as a huge market[40]. The introduction of a new trend of economic diplomacy in Indian foreign policy began with the new LPG reforms[41]. His government brought realism to the vanguard in the country's foreign policy and attempted to enhance India's ties with its neighbors through the "Look East Policy"[42]. He carried out the required modifications to assure that India was acknowledged as a major power. His experience as the MEA minister had enabled him to drive through the foreign policy reforms without vexing global or regional powers[43]. He was the predominant architect of the economic reforms that transformed India's fate forever, steering in a course of a tremendous shift. He altered India his five-year term in areas of the economy, welfare, national security and foreign policy[44]. If Nehru 'discovered' India, and if Indira Gandhi made it 'proud', Rao 'transformed it'[45]. He persists to be a captivating reminder of a crucial phase in independent India's expedition besides delivering transformational administration at a most unstable period in the country's economic history, which will stay as his calling card for the country[46]. His successor Gujral articulated a new framework for India's regional policy. Though his PM term was short-lived, the "Gujaral Doctrine" is a vital foreign policy initiative to accomplish better ties with bordering nations and to ensure harmony in South Asia, which built confidence in the diplomatic association between India and her neighbors that provide a key to bilateral matters through bilateral discussions and a pacifist manner. The following doctrine sought to conclude India's ongoing contestations with bordering nations and proposed to tread the extra mile in fixing longstanding concerns.

Vajpayee as the succeeding PM comprehended his foreign policy principles were based on the bigger angle of the Rashtriya Swayamsevak Sangh (RSS) thought on IR and courses in which he passed from it. He emerged as a personality in the classical tradition of 19th-century European strategists such as Robert Stewart, Klemens von Metternich and Lord Castlereagh, a realist dedicated to balance and restraint[47]. His foreign policy game was directed by the dawn of realism and fortified through optimism within the Indian context. He gave a structural resilience to the country's ties with China placing off a quid pro quo in Sikkim and Tibet, formalizing the territory disputes within a certain representative mechanism[48]. Also, his ties with Russia and U.S remained steady. Concerning the "Neighborhood policy", Vajpayee cast goodwill and cordiality. The key to his foreign policy was his period as MEA minister from 1977 to 1979[49]. He likewise sought two significant initiatives regularizing ties with China and Pakistan. He used back-channel diplomacy and capitalized on Pakistan's wish to host a successful SAARC summit[50]. However, he pursued to overlook Pakistan and deal directly with the Kashmiri militants but these numerous measures could not generate anticipated results[51]. He was explicit that India stays earmarked to continue with the economic liberalization agenda at a rate and in a way that one believes is ably fitted to the requirements[52]. Henceforth, besides realism, Vajpayee was embedded in the Indian milieu, its civilization, culture, values, society and customs[53]. India started self-consciously to seek 'soft power' as Nye defined it, in the last half of the 1990s. In this context, Vajpayee put efforts on nation branding, partially with FDI and tourism in sense, besides extrapolating a new idea of India globally. For instance, The "Incredible India" movement that started in 2002 is certainly one of the best known and successful of such endeavors[54]. He was considered a liberal in the Indian mind while being very distinct from the classical western liberal as described by Rousseau, Locke and John Stuart Mill[55].

Subsequently, the next PM, Manmohan Singh articulated that his United Progressive Government (UPA) aimed to fundamentally reset India's foreign policy that would be established on the country's priorities and its role in foreign affairs. His main foreign policy development was signing the land-mark civil nuclear deal[56]. Singh engaged with three subsequent governments in Pakistan and made many peace warm-ups. Also, several confidence-building measures were put in place to keep the status quo along the LAC under two different regimes in China. Theorists of IR regard Singh's worldview as realism influenced with idealism[57]. While the doctrine focuses on India's immediate developmental requirements and aim, it acknowledges the universal bearing of the importance that represents the Indian republic secularism, liberalism and pluralism in this contemporary period of populace power[58]. The "Manmohan Doctrine" therefore backed India's ties with the International powers as well as neighborhood nations, set by development priorities.

Furthermore, PM Modi regime focused on the lifeline of India's foreign policy and its strategic culture[59]. His regime that took over the office in 2014 emphasized the realignment of Indian foreign policy importance and objectives[60]. Due to India's rise, there are new directions for the government to recreate a more considerable function in regional and international governance. The elevation of the BJP and its emergence as the prominent stake of Indian foreign policy has pivoted domestic politics and the foreign policy discourse in reinvigorated approaches[61]. Strong diplomacy strives for a more incredible international impression. He is driven by nationalism that has cultural and economic elements and correspondingly moved to make economic diplomacy a more prominent priority of the MEA and India's overseas missions[62]. Modi marketed "Brand India" to the broader world rather than imaginatively[63]. Furthermore, a legible measure is underway to increase India's brand value overseas, which is possible to have important implications for the conduct of Indian diplomacy and the more comprehensive part of India in international politics in the forthcoming years[64]. A noteworthy strand of the Modi foreign policy has been a meticulous fostering of significant power ties and proficient leadership of an ever-shifting international and regional balance of power in Asia and beyond[65]. Modi's shift away from Nehru's legacy is a critical departure from the traditional foreign policy strategy of New Delhi[66].

His commitment to "religious diplomacy" likewise has been recognized as one of the unexplored parts of his conduct of India's foreign associations[67]. Modi has used religious symbols, texts, concepts and sites eminently as part of diplomacy. For example, Modi gave copies of the Bhagavad Gita to Obama, Xi Jinping and Shinzo Abe during several state visits[68]. The economic nationalist agenda 'India first' shaped Modi's attempted reinvention of foreign policy[69]. 'Panchamrit' therefore changed foreign policy into a central tool to acknowledge the national dream of India's advancement as a robust and respectable global power[70]. He aimed at resetting affinities in South Asia as a priority and sought to reinvent Indian foreign policy by substituting an older picture with a new strategy leveled not in pragmatism or even realism, but Hindu nationalist doctrine[71]. In short, Modi desired a foreign policy shaped by India's civilizational ethos[72] that denotes a constructivist approach. Like Singh too, but certainly furthermore like Gujral and Vajpayee, Modi vowed to focus on India's near neighborhood on enhancing bilateral relations with each South Asian state, on boosting connectivity between them[73]. He therefore displayed both realism and constructivism in his foreign policy approach. For instance, during the Raisina dialogue in 2017, he committed to a strategy-oriented realism, coexistence, cooperation and partnership. Later, at the Shangri la dialogue, this philosophy had softened into five S's: Samvaad ('dialogue), Samman (respect), Sahyog (cooperation), Samriddhi (prosperity) and Shanti (peace)[74].

The first hundred days of diplomacy increased the expectancy that Modi's diplomatic skills would be an asset to him[75]. While the diplomatic hop was conducted on thin ice and his ability was yet to be proved[76]. Modi took with him Nehru's dream of Asian solidarity and if Rajiv Gandhi rediscovered the Indian diaspora and the following governments competed with each other to boost it, Modi made it a focused concern in India's diplomacy[77]. According to him, "Make in India" and "Digital India" are prospects globally to elevate India and emanate benefits for themselves[78]. Modi's targeted on three fundamental elements of India's foreign policy conduct such as a multipolar world order, the great power recognition, and the Act East policy that shows the India vision ought to be perceived within the global domain[79]. Furthermore, Modi elevated the role of diplomacy with the world leaders through "Hug diplomacy" and "Selfie diplomacy". Likewise, 'Namaste diplomacy' and 'Medical diplomacy' post-COVID-19 has come to have a global acceptance that has further elevated India's soft power status[80]. Modiplomacy is correspondingly moving in several directions dealing with international matters via a series of bilateral ties and interventions at the multilateral platforms.

2.3. Role of Private Sector, Think Tanks, Universities and International Organizations in Indian Foreign Policy

The role of the private sector has a part in the arrangement of the Indian foreign policy that would not have originated before 1990[81]. The function of representative institutions such as the Federation of Indian chambers of commerce and Industry (FICCI) and Confederation of Indian Industry (CII) in its earlier manifestation as the Association of Indian Engineering Industry (AIEI) and the Associated Chambers of Commerce and Industry of India (ASSOCHAM) was also rather border-line[82]. There was also an expansion of the Indian private sector in other nations and the advancement of Indian multinational companies (MNCs).

India further started to embrace a more dynamic and proactive function in multilateral trade negotiations and evolved more accommodative towards the construction of regional trade blocs such as the SAARC and entered into other regional and bilateral free trade agreements (FTAs) and broad economic collaboration agreements[83]. Given the direction of the increasing percentage of the private sector in economic stir and its rising stakes in accessing overseas markets, technologies and economic aids, the position of the private sector in the country's foreign policy are only likely to expand[84]. The commencement of the private sector's impact on the Indian foreign economic and commercial policy can be traced back to the mid-1980s when the Rajiv Gandhi government initiated economic liberalization[85]. Under PM Vajpayee government, when Pokhran II took place, the country encountered global economic sanctions of government ties with major powers[86]. The role of the Track II diplomacy in this context by the private sector came to the vanguard. The National Democratic Alliance (NDA) government was more open-minded and receptive to the private sector's involvement and ideas in articulating its overseas commercial and economic policies[87]. The role of the private sector in essentially all significant foreign economic foreign policy matters like the Doha round of the World Trade Organization (WTO) negotiations, Indo-U.S track II dialogue, International climate change negotiations, and bilateral and regional trade negotiations was supporting of and additional to the afoot high-level government to government exchange[88]. Economic diplomacy has consistently been crucial to Indian foreign policy. The country's private sector has lobbied for the state to drive its cause with global trading and investment counterparts. For instance, the FICCI and CII have sought GOI help via engagement with the Indian diaspora.

Today, MEA and the nodal ministries involved have bolstered support and lending ties and cooperation with organizations such as the SAARC, International Monetary Fund (IMF), World Bank, The Asian Infrastructure Investment Bank (AIIB), Shanghai Cooperation Organization (SCO), Brazil, Russia, India, China, and South Africa (BRICS), New Development Bank (NDB) and G-20. Both UPA and NDA governments have energetically performed an influential in economic foreign policy success. However, as economic diplomacy has become an important segment of Indian foreign policy, intern-ministerial cooperation by the successive governments in the future can further advance the Indian foreign policy via the private sector.

Also, the role of Indian think tanks and universities have enabled in shaping policy at some key points in the history of independent India on most events they have demonstrated less influence than might have been anticipated[89]. Unfortunately, the universities have failed to produce International Studies researchers qualified of contributing to policy-making in contrast to the U.S, where foreign policy officials sometimes communicate with IR scholars in think tanks and universities by noting down their suggestions[90]. It is seen that some of these scholars also at times occupy senior administration roles in many U.S governmental departments unlike in India where bureaucrats and diplomats hardly consult the think tanks and academic institutions in constructing policy initiatives[91]. Nevertheless, this might be changing in the present circumstances due to increased cooperation between government officials and non-state actors at conferences and think tanks such as Observer Research Foundation (ORF), ICWA, the Gateway house etc. The conferences presently also bring together scholars from across India to discuss issues of IR and its methodology. The Institute for Defence Studies and Analyses (IDSA) set up in 1965 post the Sino-India war of 1962 is viewed as the country's leading think tank on strategic matters[92]. The general public is often confused about what a think tank is and how it differs from a university[93]. The quality of research in think tanks concerning foreign affairs is also mixed besides adequate funding and below the global standards in comparison to other Asian nations and the west[94]. In the recent past, the MEA has put forth the proactive PDD that has sponsored occasional Track II dialogues to help promote bilateral ties at turbulent times but much remains to be done and the university system in India also demands significant amelioration[95].

2.4 Beyond the Borders: The Contemporary Diplomacy of India

2.4.1 Para-Diplomacy: Democratization of Foreign Policy in India

Diplomacy is not just carried out by experienced diplomatic instruments. Other administrators and private individuals under the administrator's guidance conduct diplomacy. Nonetheless, during the contemporary era, in the outcome of diplomatic activities, diplomacy is more engaged with increasingly miscellaneous power and actors[96]. Actors in the field IR and diplomacy have been altered and those who play a part in the relations between other nations or other actors overseas also develop and can be accomplished by those to who the main government has given control or authority[97]. Cities are the age-old political entities and have performed a critical political function until the middle ages when the nation-state's inception in the 1500s pared them to rather minor political performers. As in diplomacy concerning state actors, power is substantial in upholding bargaining with other countries. Henceforth, soft power and hard power are the primary things in the association between regions abroad, which is known as Para diplomacy[98].

The concept of Para diplomacy in the domain of IR and foreign policymaking is a distinguishable trend globally in the contemporary era. Para diplomacy relates to the engagements of sub-national states in foreign policymaking means[99]. This concept is also comprehended as 'continent diplomacy', 'state diplomacy', 'regional diplomacy', and 'subnational diplomacy'[100]. The sub-national governments, therefore, conduct Para diplomacy, by introducing the concept of decentralization of political power to make regional governments principal actors in the global sphere[101]. Subnational diplomacy, from an academic viewpoint is of a current origin[102]. The rise of Para diplomacy should not be seen as a displacement of the state but as its complement[103]. In the study of IR, traditional schools consider states as authentic subjects, being the sole ones that maintain sovereignty, allowing them to engage sovereign states in the domain of diplomacy[104]. John Kincaid, an American scholar who outlined a foreign policy role for sub-national states in a constitutional federal system, originally presented this concept in 1990 and popularized it in the U.S following the 1970s[105].

Following the Independence, India followed NAM and a dynamic foreign policy to expand its growth transforming from a regional power to global power[106]. The Constitution of India was constructed with the intent of a robust union government and the capacity to drive foreign policy endeavors persists to stay under the exclusive responsibility of the union government[107]. Also, the trade, commerce, foreign affairs with other nations besides import and export are the realms where solely the Union ministry is responsible to legislate[108]. After the implementation of the economic liberalization of 1991, the LPG model earmarked a considerable part in carrying the practice of Para diplomacy ahead which furthermore achieved a footmark in the country through cross border actions in the area of the financial market, technology, education and information[109]. Indian states following the economic reforms of the 1990s have broadly contributed to India's foreign policy decision-making in two vital areas, which are framing India's foreign policy with its neighbors and economic diplomacy[110]. In late 1970s, coalition politics directed to mushrooming of regional parties that brought in substantial developments. The idea of liberalization would not have been achievable without the effectual association of states. India foremost began its functions in the power sector to private foreign investors when the Maharashtra government approved with Texas electric giant, Enron, and General Electric to finance its Dabhol Project in 1992[111].

India is one of the most influential and significant nations globally today and being multifarious, the nation can make use of its possibilities and techniques in conducting Para diplomacy. Former late PM Nehru in the past had written letters to the CMs explaining certain aspects of foreign policy but did not solicit their views. Later, as regional parties began to exert influence at the national level, states began to dictate terms even in foreign policy. Indian states, since the last few years have been performing a more comprehensive part in establishing sub-regional initiatives and have more incredible leeway in shaping the agenda of regional cooperation[112]. PM Modi also demonstrated a paradigm shift in the country's foreign policy-making by valuing the integral function that states can recreate in the conduct of diplomacy[113]. He further announced integrating the association of regional states in the foreign policy-making process in 2014. The "States Division" established by MEA in the same year seeks to administer states and Union

Territories (UTs) by communicating with them in areas such as commerce, investment, culture and so on[114]. Former Joint Secretary in the States Division of the MEA, Gopal Baglay, emphasized that increased relations of states in the context of the conduct of foreign matters would usher in cooperative and competitive federalism[115]. This is also arising as a distinguished example of "cooperative federalism", putting large priority on states acting as equal partners in the growth of the country in the diplomatic areas of FDI, trade, cultural and educational exchanges [116]. It would indeed make the states and cities have the chance to generate a remarkable affinity with nations or federal states or even cities of their interest.

India can help by putting the country's federal states on the global map and should consider taking thoughts from cities like Macau, Sao Paulo and New York that have been thriving in Para diplomacy[117]. GOI intends to improve Indian commissions overseas, altering them into industry and finance centers by connecting a more central role for the states in Indian foreign policy[118]. An important element of Para diplomacy, "Indian diaspora" can further aid to contribute via Para diplomacy in myriad forms for their states like the Tamil diaspora in Singapore, Telugu diaspora in the U.S etc.[119] The notion of "Maritime Paradiplomacy" is another sub-national construct of developing overseas links on nautical lines through India's maritime federal states as the country already possess a 7416.6 km coastline[120]. For instance, the Alappuzha Heritage Project in the state of Kerala is supported by Netherlands and strives to direct the protection and conservation agenda via historical channels and hinterland connectivity[121].

Flourishing Para diplomacy results in investment, employment creation and possibly the reputation of delivering a well-known brand. Foreign investments, digital India, make-in-India, smart cities mission such as the ASEAN smart cities network and good governance initiatives have additionally aided in boosting Para diplomacy. Even major investment summits such as the "Vibrant Gujarat" are a good example of Para diplomacy[122]. Also, importantly, the Northeast region (NER) of India has facilitative geography and closeness to the markets of ASEAN countries has boosted its economic Para diplomacy with neighboring countries. Hazarika's *"Paradigms of Para-diplomacy in the Northeast"* describes the Para diplomatic measures made by these NER states, with a particular focus on Assam, which directs to the "Act East Policy"[123]. Kurian, a scholar of Asian boundaries and regionalism states that NER must host operating parties involving regional organizations such as Bangladesh, China, India and Myanmar Economic Corridor (*BCIM*) and BIMSTEC on various issues[124]. As the role of NER has increased in the last decade, its role becomes vital in the realm of Para diplomacy and Indian foreign policy as well.

Furthermore, the CMs of states like Kerala, West Bengal, Gujarat, Andhra Pradesh, Rajasthan, Chattisgarh, Telangana and Tamil Nadu have conducted the role of "Chief-diplomat" in promoting the Para diplomacy with several countries[125]. One well-known example is that of the former CM of Andhra Pradesh, Chandrababu Naidu witnessed media and academic attention by taking benefit of shifts in the country's liberalizing economy to pursue help from global investors and resource donors for his state. Following (Rudolph & Rudolph, 2001) it would be pertinent to organize Naidu's diplomatic technique as entrepreneurial[126]. The incorporation of Chief Ministers (CMs) in PM dialogues overseas is a modern practice in India's foreign ties[127]. Yet, CMs have encountered financial hardships as the center changed the rules for administering resources and commitments, prompting them to pursue FDI to bolster their state economies[128]. CMs hold influential commitments in the Indian federal system of government. Yet their political survival is not assured if the benefits of office are not skillfully utilized[129]. Furthermore, post-COVID pandemic, the centre-state ties have been strained.

As India's positing is ascending on the international podium, its states will remain to have an augmented role in foreign policy prospects. Though Para diplomacy in India is still in its developing phase, the state, as an actor and topic of study, will persist to be paramount to comprehend the global arena. The states must therefore acquire expertise in IR to make responsible decisions in their relations with overseas countries[130]. India should enrich its Para diplomacy via the conception of consulates in regional states, founding federal foreign affairs offices under the authority of the MEA[131]. Para diplomacy can further amplify the federal structure of GOI and also rationalize the foreign policy strategy by supporting regional governments to acknowledge their potential in the conduct of cross-border ties. Though MEA has established a 'states division', the union government must also link in a more suitable approach and institute transparency to view the developments of pursuing Para diplomacy. Also, a states division in the MEA cannot make a difference in foreign policy and state policy-making[132]. A fresh arrangement or design, in which Indian states are comprehensively represented, should be set up where the MEA should have offices in pivotal states[133]. The inclusion of Public-private partnership (PPP) in foreign projects in regional states should be given importance apart from establishing think tanks or NGOs in states to foster policy alternatives and to deliver information to the states and the center[134]. The states must also develop expertise in foreign affairs to be able to take responsible decisions in their interaction with foreign lands and India must learn from the success of countries like China and the U.S that have successfully harnessed Para diplomacy. The role of states is therefore crucial and driving their economic advantage would recreate an essential part in the rise of India besides elevating state and civil society interaction, leveraging the soft power and foreign policy making which can furthermore contribute to the country's co-operative federalism and five trillion dollar economy. Nevertheless, even if the Para diplomatic shifting resumes to grow, both in the spectrum and in the profoundness of matters, the GOI will remain to be the primary player in foreign affairs[135].

2.5.2 Public Diplomacy: The New Age Diplomacy

The belief of man being a political animal has been well created by the Greek philosopher, Aristotle. Living in a closed interwoven societal setup, humans have advanced in the political, economic political and social associations[136]. Nation-states have become a part of the global dynamics that are bound to be part of the dialogue exchanges affecting events besides observing global affairs. This exchange of dialogues is termed "diplomacy" that has been a vital part of IR, which connects the international actors. Diplomacy has therefore been a vital part of IR, as it is what makes it about links between international actors. A well-known example is the U.N, which is primarily known as an IOs while considering diplomacy. U.N has been involved in multilateral, public, conference or parliamentary diplomacy[137].

The phrase "PD" was first invented by the scholars at Tufts University in the mid-1960s for explaining the effects of IR on the U.S[138]. Undoubtedly, soft power has become the primary tool in public diplomacy. Factors that have nurtured public diplomacy in India include a robust economy, unparalleled soft power, domestic front, powerful Indian diaspora and consular diplomacy[139]. Therefore, PD is an essential means to project a nation's soft power towards the global society as it involves actions usually under-taken by a national administration to advise and impact foreign public opinion and perspectives to promote its foreign policy pursuits[140]. The fundamental pillars of soft power according to Nye are foreign policy, culture and political values. It has been rare to see successful foreign policies solely established on the concept of hard power resources. They emphasize where the state interests come from as against the Realists who take state interests as given[141]. The foreign policy of a country is furthermore a social construction of actuality and PD constitutes an essential part of a country's foreign policy[142]. New PD has emphasized the effectiveness of "soft power," the ability to exercise power through the force of beliefs, organizations, values, and civilization[143]. Also, Indian foreign aid is a reflection of its strategic interests and self-perception as the major regional power and an emerging international power. The country's foreign aid depicts the prominent position entrusted to this soft power tool of Indian foreign policy[144].

Today, numerous governments implement soft power more than hard power while conducting IR. This is because a nation cannot depend on hard power independently and that's when soft power aspects play a crucial part in maintaining bilateral relations. According to Nye, due to the distribution of power between state actors and non-state actors, non-state actors like big firms, NGOs, and the media decide a nation's soft power[145]. The majority of the nations likewise depend on what is known as 'Smart Power', which includes both hard power and soft power[146]. Due to the bipolar system of IR, countries have primarily played the role of fundamental actors in PD implementation tools[147]. Nye within the framework of the theory of IR has considered PD through the prism of the soft power phenomenon[148]. Traditional diplomacy has focused on engaging the government officials and state actors in the diplomatic process. However, PD contributes to the development of dialogue with foreign counterparts through the means of involvement of non-official resources[149]. On several occurrences, Nye stressed the significance of comprehending other individuals as recipients of information and also engaged players of multilateral communications[150]. Furthermore, modern PD has been greatly affected by the technological aspects delivering for gradual advancement of the image of the state and phenomenal improvement of study in the domain of informational-communicational technologies and contemporary media[151]. Architects of the PD approach attribute a much more noteworthy role to such elements of soft power as the collection of cultural values, accomplishments in the sphere of increased technologies, the attraction of ideological part and the interpretation of socio-economic[152].

The concept of foreign policy has likewise used the term "PD" along with the concept of "social diplomacy" as it is regarded as appropriate to acknowledge that the activities of the NGOs to a more significant extent come within the coverage of the purpose of social diplomacy[153]. Furthermore, the fundamental mechanism included in PD measures is the media that can influence individuals' opinions and thoughts greatly. PD, over time, has become varnished and is now implied in the diplomatic sense concerning the general public[154]. The characterization of the whole diplomatic process is disseminated by media to the people and therefore, media has a paramount intermediary part in PD[155]. Thriving implementation of PD directs approval and support from the state actors as well in realizing their interests and goals[156].

2.5.2.1 Public Diplomacy in India

PD is a step to encourage favorable bilateral ties with the public of another nation besides winning the minds and hearts of the people of another nation. It seeks to foster positive relations via NGOs, media, education exchange programs etc. The NGOs is especially important in shaping the new way of PD[157]. India's PD efforts included outreach to developed nations by running a global 'Incredible India' tourism campaign, founding business councils and chambers of commerce and hosting global exhibitions to brand India by marketing the country's image overseas[158]. In Asia, China pioneered the usage of PD to construct the national stature in the global arena following which Japan (2004), Malaysia (2006), and India (2006) set special divisions within their foreign ministries to craft novel PD agendas[159]. However, scholars such as Sandre & Seib delivered necessary commentaries on how PD ought to be conducted, but they do not assess its function in the social media sphere, particularly in the context of South Asia[160]. India's growing power has been the topic of much discussion and dialogue among academics, state and media following the end of the cold war. The study of the country's public diplomacy is a rather contemporary outfit although the course has dated back to the duration of former PM Nehru who strived to construct a distinctive essence for the nation highlighting norms and values such as NAM, decolonization and development partnerships[161]. According to Navtej Suri, former Indian diplomat, the elements of PD include digital diplomacy, projection of soft power, image and branding, constructing a positive narrative, broadcasting, coordination and strategic communications[162]. Also, the main establishments involved in the country's PD abroad are the External Publicity and Public Diplomacy (XPD) Division, Overseas Indian Affairs (OIA) Division, and the Development Partnership Administration (DPA) Division that operate under MEA[163]. The country's independent organizations such as ICCR and ICWA furthermore perform an important part in PD[164].

PD is a necessary vehicle to disseminate India's purposes to the global community[165]. It's measures concentrate on accentuating the fact that the government seeks dialogue, engagement, partnership and accommodation wherever feasible. The objective is to assure that established powers will not adopt obstructionist standings due to India's increasing aspirations[166]. India aspires to ensure the global society that it will not seek use force against its neighbors and other nations. Furthermore, India's PD measures aim to persuade the world that the government is unlikely to engage in military or economic disputes. PD measures are devised to minimize anxiety and opposition to India's aspirations by communicating the message that a rising India will not function like other rising powers in history. India's aspirations of great power status and rising competition with other nations are pushing the country to adopt PD as an influential segment of its foreign policy. Nevertheless, it is anticipated that the spirit and range of PD will continue to grow in India. The country will not undermine IOs and vows to support the existent international order, founded on the twin pillars of liberal democracy and free trade. India's view that it is likely to reform contemporary IOs, such as the IMF, UNSC, World Bank and WTO to deliver a more important function not just to it but also to other nations in the developing world, will likewise prove advantageous to others as they strive to address the nation's evolving aspirations. Soft power is notoriously hard to translate into a clear diplomatic benefit[167]. To conduct PD, Indian diplomats ought to create better connections with the broader foreign policy society in India, specifically with universities and think tanks[168].

Culture is at the core of India's practice of PD in the 21st century[169]. Unfortunately, India's image is undermined by red tape, levels of bureaucratic inertia, social inequality, human rights violations, gender and caste violence, poor governance and corruption which challenge India's claims of being a rising power with aspirations of great power status[170]. Besides, the unwillingness of foreign policy officials and some politicians and professionals to engage with foreign audiences and disseminate India's opinions and standings on significant global problems is another impediment to the thriving behavior of PD[171]. Lack of funding for MEA division XPD has been a drawback even though the state and the bureaucracy are essential players in the exercise of successful PD[172].

PD despite its challenges remains an important tool in the foreign policy of GOI to improve its influence and power globally besides being a target-oriented activity in terms of purposes and audience[173]. Furthermore, it can accomplish just specific targets, as internal polarities of a nation especially of a democratic polity like India cannot be concealed[174]. However, it cannot be solely an afterthought though it has to become critical at all levels of foreign policymaking. Therefore, for India to become a prominent power globally, GOI has to influence all resources of soft power where PD is an essential one[175]. Funding can be expanded in cultural activities in Indian embassies and consulates can further expand Indian PD[176]. India should also boost its academic and professional exchange programs with IOs and universities apart from inviting distinguished members of CSOs of other nations to promote a better sense of Indian civilization, interests and values that can depict India in an optimistic glare[177]. The Indian diplomacy that is moving towards initiatives like PD with a considerable understanding of social constructivism in a changing world should therefore maintain a balance between flexibility and transparency by coming out of its stereotypes and obsolete standards.

2.5.3. Digital Diplomacy in India

Diplomacy has been an integral part of IR, as it is what causes its associations between international actors. Another important way to connect digitally is due to the era of technology, named the "digital revolution" which has greatly impacted all elements of life such as global ties. There has been expanded academic interest in "DD" in the past decade with scholars considering the digital approaches of state officials and global leaders. The realms of diplomacy and governance have been altered by technology[178]. Diplomatic engagements that presently define digital presence are bilateral and multilateral relations, consular services, image formation, social engagement, promotion, public diplomacy, use of ICT and internal administrative procedures[179]. DD is the art of soft power in this globalized world, integrating the traditional methods of diplomatic approach and the negotiation and ability to bind power that is marked by advancing technologies and innovation[180]. It is on its path to overcoming the hurdles fronted by traditional diplomatic practices[181]. The world is getting revolutionized in the modern day with technology in play, making life easy and has connected nearly all areas of human life[182]. Diplomacy via the advancement of technology has made social media an effective medium in daily diplomatic matters making it better transparent and accessible. Therefore, DD and social media can jointly contribute to establishing and disseminating a nation's foreign policy importance to domestic and foreign audiences[183]. DD has led to a normative shift for diplomats to embrace a new kind of openness due to the heightened agency of non-state actors such as CSOs, NGOs etc. which led to a subsequent metamorphosis in diplomats' conduct as they currently seek to construct interim associations, or networks, to promote distinctive objectives[184].

Contemporary years have seen expanded academic Interest in the confluence between diplomacy and digital technologies[185]. Scholars have considered diplomats' usage of digital means to engage with new audiences, overcome the constraint of traditional diplomacy, cooperate with new players and foster cross-cultural discussion[186]. Though digital diplomacy cannot substitute the conventional way of diplomacy, the former and the latter can complement and go face to face with each other which can create an all-around influence in constructing India's image and its foreign policy[187].

Henceforth, 2017 marks a decade since the advent of "DD"[188]. The discussion of DD globally is nonetheless in the beginning that has evolved into a significant movement by catching up with nations that have already fared well in digital diplomacy[189]. Diplomacy in India has lauded technological shifts as diplomats, different ministries, and political heads have been in acceptance of social media to conduct diplomacy. India has cooperated with private industry to facilitate its outreach efforts.

India is aspiring to be a trendsetter, by carving its way to being an international leader. Social media in India allows encouraging communication about its coming of age through scientific advancement, technological accomplishments, contemporary ideas that have taken ahead in recent years besides acting as a stimulant in social activism[190]. Indian diplomacy is the ideal of the constructivist approach of diplomacy, highlighting ideas, values and most notably soft power. It has positively welcomed technological changes as several ministries, diplomats and political leaders have adopted social media to practice diplomacy[191]. Foreign ministries globally urge their diplomats to utilize social media within their traditional communication approaches[192]. The MEA has been the leader in the use of technology such as social media platforms and was rated among the top 10 foreign affairs ministries in the use of social media in diplomatic methods and engaging with people[193]. MEA's DD endeavor in the recent years has been incredible in shaping foreign policy and creating a robust and efficient web with the people. An important example is the 'SAMEEP – Students and MEA Engagement Programme', an initiative to promote young bright minds across India that will also serve to bring closer the Indian public to the foreign policy of India. The aim is to acquaint school and college students with the functions and role of MEA, fundamental elements of the country's foreign policy besides its achievements[194]. After the MEA established its website in 2003, its online presence has expanded phenomenally and its Twitter handles such as @IndianDiplomacy, IndiaInitiative@Davos and @MEAIndia has nearly 3.0 million followers as per the MEA yearly report of 2017-2018. The Indian missions have become digital and are energetically articulating or communicating with people in host nations and importantly the diaspora[195]. The Indian missions have Facebook presence under labels such as "India in Ireland", "India in the USA" etc. besides regular updates being disseminated on investment, prospects, embassy activities and flagship endeavors such as "Invest India", "Skill India", "Make in India", "Digital India" etc. [196] MEA's online presence has played a crucial part in numerous crisis events and was conducive during evacuation measures from countries like Libya, Nepal and Yemen[197]. For some of the rising powers like India that has been former colonies, social media is a great instrument for reversing unfavorable impressions and demonstrating positive credentials with the developed world. The MEA through DD has significantly assisted in molding the foreign policy and constructing a robust web with the public and Indian diaspora who play an essential function in the Indian foreign policy.

International leaders and state officials have gone digital and more than 67% of all the state leaders and over 3,500 ambassadors and embassies have Twitter accounts, taking to social media with enthusiasm[198]. Diplomacy in India is the epitome of the constructivist perspective of diplomacy, emphasizing concepts, values, ideals and particularly soft power[199]. After the U.S state department amongst foreign ministries, MEA's official Facebook page stands second with more than 1.2 million followers[200]. Therefore, the digital shift shows that India is steering into the future at an exceptional pace by taking the digital gateway to link with the world efficiently. The U.S Department of State has been seen as the forefront of digital diplomacy that refers to as 21st century statecraft, utilizing new technology to engage a growing, transforming set of stakeholders globally[201].

The digital revolution notwithstanding its challenges has influenced all walks of life including IR. However, barriers like counter propaganda and disinformation by non-state actors and governments have risen presently for strategic interests that have led to serious insinuation for global order. Cyber security is also a major challenge as several Indian governmental websites have been prone to hacking and leaking of information[202]. Indian state should experiment with new things in improving the digital diplomatic foothold. Also, India would benefit much from more global platforms to engage international audiences and convey not just what India has to present the world in terms of its broader cultural proposals, but also represent its aspirations, importance, and precise foresight for the country's promising position in the world. GOI must think outside the box on expanding its presence digitally globally and improve its budget spending to offer state of the art digital services. GOI can put in more measures to become a "Digital nation" and emanate ideas from nations like the U.S, Canada, the U.K etc. that topped the "Soft power 30" chart in the digital category[203]. The quick transformation to "zoom diplomacy" in 2020 due to the pandemic shows how these practices can temporarily replace the traditional diplomacy[204]. Therefore, DD is here to endure, evolve and innovate. It is crucial for the present and forthcoming diplomats to embrace all the roads of communication it presents.

2.6 Cultural Diplomacy in India

While there is no definite meaning of the term, American political scientist Milton C. Cummings' states that CD are the exchange of ideas, information, values, systems, traditions, beliefs, and other aspects of culture, to foster mutual understanding[205]. It is a necessary instrument in the arsenal of smart power too, but smart PD demands an awareness of the position of credibility, self-criticism, and the role of civil society in rendering soft power[206]. The emphasis on soft power, especially CD, and its use in foreign policy, has become increasingly visible in recent years. Using culture as a means of diplomacy holds importance by creating ties in humanitarian settings, which leads to long-term associations because of the kind of trust that is imbibed which has furthermore helped the Indian foreign policy[207].

The use of culture as soft power diplomacy has very quickly enabled India to show an image at the international forum besides continuing to bolster the country's function as a fundamental stakeholder in global politics. The MEA and ministry of culture are responsible to a great extent for the promotion of CD. The consciousness of the significance of using culture as a means of soft power diplomacy struck post Independence and the ICCR was set up in 1950 as a nodal body. The latest in India's soft power is the "Ramayana Diplomacy"[208]. The genuine importance of lord Rama in India's IR may have recently started[209]. Nevertheless, the Ramayana epic has reached various corners of the world in the previous many centuries as part of the nation's soft power[210]. In India, Rama is, therefore regarded as the thread of 'unity in diversity. The Ramayana is simplistic, yet provides the holy guidebook of the country[211].

Following the pandemic in 2020, PM Boris Johnson of the U.K after inaugurating the virtual Diwali fest announced that the country will defeat COVID-19 like the way Lord Rama and Sita defeated Ravana (an important character in the Ramayana epic)[212]. Also, the Brazilian President Bolsonaro wrote to PM Modi about Ramayana and compared India's effort to contain the pandemic to Hanuman and 'Sanjeevani Booti' (a lithophytic plant used for medicinal purposes found in India)[213]. GOI has been trying to reinvigorate the mythical epic in multiple ways via media and diplomacy and to enrich the Ramayana spirit, GOI has additionally identified 15 destinations in India for the development as part of the 'Ramayana Circuit' theme under the Swadesh Darshan scheme via the Tourism ministry[214]. Ramayana has materialized as captivating representations of an effective cultural association, connecting South Asia, South East Asia and India[215]. GOI further offers to establish a 'Group of Ramayana' nations for a soft-power diplomacy push[216]. However, Ramayana diplomacy will take time to mature, as some of India's neighbors remain to be anxious beyond lands and boundaries[217].

Significantly since PM Modi came to power in 2014, there has been advanced activism to attract attention to and employ India's soft power though Nehru also stressed on soft power in the past. Today, besides Ayurveda, Indian films, tourism and music, yoga has achieved tremendous respect from different nations where the GOI has been contributing a lot to promote yoga globally through "CD". Yoga is periodically assumed as a religious act mostly confined to Hinduism exclusively. Whereas the UN General Assembly (UNGA) resolution disproved these views and demonstrated the importance of yoga for the mental, physical, and spiritual well being of all people. GOI lately announced the establishment of an independent Ministry for Yoga, which is a welcome decision. The proposed ministry should in the process cooperate with the Ministry of Human Resources and Development (HRD) to facilitate institutional partnerships at the global level to further promote the study and practice of yoga in overseas universities[218]. The ICCR has also disbursed funds to India's more than 170 diplomatic missions to celebrate the occasion in 2021[219].

The Indian diaspora, an important segment of India's soft power today plays a vital role in heightening the cultural diplomacy. Diaspora is known to be influential stakeholders of history and civilization that have emerged as a productive core due to their tangible proof of perception as 'Soft Power' in the realm of foreign policy maneuvering. Diaspora bolsters and embodies both tangible and intangible culture within the cores of migration. The India Diaspora is considered as the most prominent diaspora and constitutes an integral and unique force in the global economy and has retained its cultural, vibrant and spiritual associations with the country of origin. Indian Diaspora namely NRIs and PIOs play an integral function in projecting its Soft Power. Though the foreign networks are sources of trade, remittances, assets and brain banks on the other side India experiences brain drain and scarce talent. Nevertheless, GOI through MEA has thus brought in various initiatives to enlarge its soft power diplomacy such as Pravasi Bharatiya Divas, 'Know India' etc. By 2024, U.N has indicated that India will become the most populous country globally and therefore the Indian diaspora will continue to grow. The diaspora are indeed a tool for 'soft power diplomacy' for its retention of cultural richness of India. They have been bridges, mediators, facilitators, lobby and advocacy groups for taking primacy of India's' national security and economic interests. India can harness upon its well-exposed diaspora youth and make them partners for raising India's human capital. Therefore, with the increasing diaspora, it is India's responsibility to nurture, understand, conserve and strengthen this heritage for the country's future generations.

2.7. Conclusion

India has continually been viewed as a "cultural superpower" with a wide reserve of soft power resources. Very few nations can match the rich history, civilization and culture of the country that constructs an exceptional attraction and charm for India overseas. The country's dynamic and flourishing democracy, its autonomous and free media, its democratic establishments and its increasingly conscious and pulsating civil society all contribute to its soft power. However, communal riots, corruption, campus protests, social and gender inequality, lack of media transparency, inefficient healthcare, pollution, vigilant attacks, news accounts etc. about the repression of minorities barely paint a portrait of a rising international power. Historian, Guha noted that because of India's size diversity and dogged poverty it remains the most impatiently ambitious historical experimentation. He further states that despite a woman serving as the PM, in some parts of India, female infanticide is still very common.

The release of the 2021 Global soft power index shows that India does not showcase in the top 20 on the index further slipping 9 places to 36th rank in 2021 from the previous year due to protests and civil unrest[220]. There has also been a decline of India's rank in nation brands index 2021 nevertheless, the index report emphasizes the country's strengths such as robust performance in heritage and culture, entertainment and arts[221]. India's economy, foreign aid to developing nations, the country's role in disaster relief and humanitarian operations has shaped and led to the elevation of the rise of India's soft power per the report[222]. Again, the attraction of India as a higher education hub for developing nations in Africa and Asia is the emerging new soft power resource[223]. The elevation of India passport index 2022 also adds to the soft power potential. Presently, the world stands at an unprecedented threshold with international power shifts taking place in the cloud of nuclear weapons. India has certainly pushed forward, but its achievements have descended shortly of its more remarkable potential. As a rising force, India is presumably to recreate a key role in shaping academic understandings of power and its limitations in the 21st century. Importantly, technological advancement such as Artificial Intelligence (AI), cyber security, robotics, nanotechnology, genetics etc. and the emergence of non-state actors key players has significantly affected Indian foreign policy and shifting character of power.

To transform the foreign policy of India, the GOI should therefore harness its soft power potential to its fullest and focus on the weak areas by learning from top soft power countries. GOI should perform a great role in enhancing governance through new age diplomacy strategies to suit the contemporary era foreign policy of India.

Notes

1. Leira (2019) The Emergence of foreign Policy, *International Studies Quarterly*, Volume 63, Issue.
2. Bojang, S. (2018) The Study of Foreign Policy in International Relations. *Journal of Political Sciences & Public Affairs*. 06. DOI: 10.4172/2332-0761.1000337.
3. Sharma. (2011) *The Shaping of India's new foreign policy*. New Delhi: VIJ Books.
4. *Ibid.*
5. *Ibid.*
6. Quinn, A. (2018) *How History Shapes India's Foreign Policy Goals.* Available at: https://www.e-ir.info/2018/08/04/how-history-shapes-indias-foreign-policy-goals/ (Accessed: 3 August 2021)
7. Mullen, R (2015) *India's soft power: Indian foreign policy*. London: Oxford university press.
8. *Ibid.*
9. *Ibid.*
10. Guha, R. (2007) *India after Gandhi*. New Delhi: Picador India.
11. *Ibid.*
12. *Ibid.*
13. *Ibid.*
14. *Ibid.*
15. *Ibid.*
16. Mohan, R. (2014) *Nehru's realism*. Available at: https://www.orfonline.org/research/nehrus-realism/ (Accessed: 3 September 2019)
17. Guha, R. (2007) *India after Gandhi.* New Delhi: Picador India.
18. *Ibid.*
19. Kennedy (2015) *Nehru's foreign policy: Indian foreign policy*. London: Oxford university press.
20. *Ibid.*
21. *Ibid.*

22. *Ibid.*
23. *Ibid.*
24. Das (2013) *India Grows At Night: A Liberal Case for a Strong State*. New York: Penguin.
25. Guha, R. (2007) *India after Gandhi.* New Delhi: Picador India.
26. Mansingh (2015) *Indira Gandhi's foreign policy: Indian foreign policy*. London: Oxford university Press.
27. *Ibid.*
28. Katju. (2022) *50 years of Indo-Soviet treaty*. Available at: https://www.tribuneindia.com/news/comment/50-years-of-indo-soviet-treaty-294975 (Accessed: 3 August 2021)
29. Mansingh (2015) *Indira Gandhi's foreign policy: Indian foreign policy*. London: Oxford university Press.
30. Cohen, S. (2002) *Emerging power: India*. Washington D.C: Brookings.
31. Bhagwati, J. (2019) *Indira Gandhi: The Promise of India: How Prime Ministers Nehru to Modi Shaped the nation (1947-2019).* New Delhi: Viking.
32. Raghavan (2015) *At the cusp of transformation: Indian foreign policy*. London: Oxford University Press.
33. *Ibid.*
34. *Ibid.*
35. *Ibid.*
36. *Ibid.*
37. *Ibid.*
38. PTI. (2021) *Narasimha Rao gave new sense of direction to economic, foreign policies, says Ex-PM Manmohan Singh*. Available at: https://indianexpress.com/article/india/narasimha-rao-birth-anniversary-manmohan-singh-7379644/ (Accessed: 17 December 2021)
39. *Ibid.*
40. *Ibid.*
41. *Ibid.*
42. *Ibid.*
43. Reddy, R (2020) *PV deserved Bharat Ratna for his foreign policy*. Available at: https://www.thehindu.com/news/cities/Hyderabad/pv-deserved-bharat-ratna-for-his-foreign-policy/article32482171.ece (Accessed: 9 February 2021)
44. Kumar, M. (2016) *Understanding P.V. Narasimha Rao*. Available at: https://www.gatewayhouse.in/half-lion-how-p-v-narasimha-rao-transformed-india/. (Accessed: 19 April 2019)
45. Dogra (2020) *Narasimha Rao: The real Chanakya: India's World: How Prime Ministers shaped Foreign policy*. New Delhi: Rupa
46. *Ibid.*
47. Rej, A. (2020) *The foreign policy legacy of Atal Bihari Vajpayee*. Available at: https://www.livemint.com/Opinion/kZI9uaKnH41oM9d7HJdfZO/The-foreign-policy-legacy-of-Atal-Bihari-Vajpayee.html (Accessed: 9 April 2021)

48. Talukdar, S (2018) *Disruptor, realist, optimist: Atal Bihari Vajpayee's foreign policy both carried forward and departed from Nehruvian legacy.* Available at: https://www.firstpost.com/india/disruptor-realist-optimist-atal-bihari-vajpayees-foreign-policy- both-carried-forward-and-departed-from-nehruvian-legacy-4993601.html (Accessed: 9 April 2021)
49. Joshi. (2018) *Vajpayee's Foreign Policy May Be His Most Enduring Legacy.* Available at: https://www.firstpost.com/india/disruptor-realist-optimist-atal-bihari-vajpayees-foreign-policy-both-carried-forward-and-departed-from-nehruvian-legacy-4993601.html (Accessed: 9 April 2021)
50. *Ibid.*
51. *Ibid.*
52. Sinha (2020) *Vajpayee: The years that changed India.* New Delhi: Penguin Random House India.
53. *Ibid.*
54. *Ibid.*
55. *Ibid.*
56. IWN (2013) A Free and Prosperous India: Five Principles of Foreign Policy. Available at: https://mea.gov.in/articles-in-indian-media.htm?dtl/22430/A+Free+and+Prosperous+India+Five+Principles+of+Foreign+Policy (Accessed: 11 April 2021)
57. Baru, S (2013), *The Singh doctrine*. Available at: https://indianexpress.com/article/opinion/columns/the-singh-doctrine/. (Accessed: 11 April 2022)
58. *Ibid.*
59. Chaulia. (2016) *Modi Doctrine: The Foreign Policy of India's Prime Minister*. New Delhi: Bloomsbury India
60. Pant, HV (2019) *New Directions in India's foreign policy: Theory and Praxis.* Cambridge: Cambridge University press
61. *Ibid.*
62. *Ibid.*
63. Pant (2019) *Indian Foreign Policy: The Modi Era.* New Delhi: Har-Anand Publications.
64. *Ibid.*
65. *Ibid.*
66. *Ibid.*
67. Hall, H. (2019) *Modi and the reinvention of Indian foreign policy*. Bristol: Bristol University Press.
68. *Ibid.*
69. *Ibid.*
70. *Ibid.*
71. *Ibid.*
72. *Ibid.*
73. *Ibid.*
74. *Ibid.*

75. Sreenivasan, T.P (2019) *Modi Storm grips India: Modiplomacy: Through a Shakespearean Prism.* New Delhi: Konark Publishers.
76. *Ibid.*
77. *Ibid.*
78. *Ibid.*
79. Ogden, C (2018) *Tone Shift: India's Dominant Foreign Policy Aims Under Modi*. Available at: Tone Shift: India's Dominant Foreign Policy Aims Under Modi, Indian politics & policy. Vol 1, No 1. Spring 2018. DOI: 10.18278/inpp.1.1.2
80. Amaresh, P. (2020) *The Good Vibes: India's Namaste Diplomacy Post-COVID-19*. Available at: https://diplomatist.com/2020/05/28/the-good-vibes-indias-namaste-diplomacy-post-covid-19/(Accessed: 9 December 2020)
81. Kumar (2015) *The private sector: Indian foreign policy*. London: Oxford university press.
82. *Ibid.*
83. *Ibid.*
84. *Ibid.*
85. *Ibid.*
86. *Ibid.*
87. *Ibid.*
88. *Ibid.*
89. Mattoo, Medcalf (2015) *Think tanks and universities: Indian foreign policy*. London: Oxford University press.
90. *Ibid.*
91. *Ibid.*
92. *Ibid.*
93. *Ibid.*
94. *Ibid.*
95. *Ibid.*
96. Ahmad et.al (2021) 'A Review of Para-diplomacy Literature: Mini-Review Approach', *Proceedings of the 11th Annual International Conference on Industrial Engineering and Operations Management,* Singapore, 7-11 March.
97. *Ibid.*
98. *Ibid.*
99. Amaresh, P (2020) *Diplomacy within Diplomacy: The Upswing of Para Diplomacy in India.* Available at: https://diplomatist.com/2020/06/01/diplomacy-within-diplomacy-the-upswing-of-para-diplomacy-in-India/ (Accessed: 2 January 2021)
100. *Ibid.*
101. Alvarez (2020) *The Rise of Para diplomacy in International Relations*. Available at: https://www.e-ir.info/2020/03/17/the-rise-of-paradiplomacy-in-international-relations/ (Accessed: 3 January 2021)
102. *Ibid.*
103. *Ibid.*

104. Tewari, F. (2017) *Para diplomacy in India: Evolution and operationalization*. ORF Occasional Paper 119. Available at: https://www.orfonline.org/research/paradiplomacy-india-evolution-Operationalization/ (Accessed: 9 April 2020)

105. Pant, Tewari. (2017) 'Para diplomacy and India: The growing role of states in Foreign policy', *LSE blog*, 12 January. Available at: https://blogs.lse.ac.uk/southasia/2017/01/12/paradiplomacy-and-india- the-growing-role-of-states-in-foreign-policy/ (Accessed: 13 April 2020)

106. Amaresh, P (2020) *Diplomacy within Diplomacy: The Upswing of Para Diplomacy in India*. Available at: https://diplomatist.com/2020/06/01/diplomacy-within-diplomacy-the-upswing-of-para-diplomacy-in-india/ (Accessed: 9 September 2020)

107. *Ibid.*

108. *Ibid.*

109. *Ibid.*

110. *Ibid.*

111. *Ibid.*

112. Girdhar, K (2021) *Para diplomacy in India: The globalism of Localism.* Available at: https://www.teenink.com/nonfiction/academic/article/1138352/Paradiplomacy-In-India-The-Globalization-Of-Localis (Accessed: 9 October 2021)

113. *Ibid.*

114. *Ibid.*

115. Khan, Mishra (2015) *Integrating Northeast in India's Act East Policy*, Sapru House, viewed 7 September 2020, ICWA, New Delhi.

116. Jacob, H (2016) *Putting the periphery at the Centre: Indian States' Role in Foreign Policy.* Available at: https://carnegieindia.org/2016/10/10/putting-periphery-at-center-Indian-states-role-in-foreign-policy-pub-64724 (Accessed: 8 September 2020)

117. Amaresh, P (2020) Diplomacy within Diplomacy: The Upswing of Para Diplomacy in India. Available at: https://diplomatist.com/2020/06/01/diplomacy-within-diplomacy-the-upswing-of-para-diplomacy-in-india/ (Accessed: 9 January 2021)

118. *Ibid.*

119. *Ibid.*

120. Vijay (2019) *Indian maritime Para diplomacy: Connecting sub-national nautical dots.* Available at: https://maritimeindia.org/indian-maritime-paradiplomacy-connecting-sub-national-nautical-dots/ (Accessed 9 February 2020)

121. Antony, T (2019) *CM Pinarayi Vijayan's Holland visit to aid Kerala's heritage projects*. Available at: https://www.newindianexpress.com/states/kerala/2019/may/10/cms-holland-visit-to-aid-states-heritage-projects-1974895.html (Accessed: 9 February 2020)

122. PTI (2021) *PM Modi to inaugurate 10th edition of Vibrant Gujarat Global Summit.* Available at: https://timesofindia.indiatimes.com/india/pm-modi-to-inaugurate-10th-edition-of-vibrant-gujarat-global-summit/articleshow/87909852.cms (Accessed: 9 February 2020)

123. Nayar, N (2021) 'Para diplomacy in Northeast India: Assam Acts East', *CSEP blog*, 11 October, Available at: https://csep.org/blog/paradiplomacy-in-northeast-india-assam-acts-east/ (Accessed 2 January 2022)
124. *Ibid.*
125. Vijay (2019) *Indian maritime Para diplomacy: Connecting sub-national nautical dots.* Available at: https://maritimeindia.org/indian-maritime-paradiplomacy-connecting-sub-national-nautical-Dots/ (Accessed 9 February 2020)
126. Wyatt, A (2017) Para-diplomacy of India's chief ministers, *India Review*, 16:1, 106-124, DOI: 10.1080/14736489.2017.1279932((
127. *Ibid.*
128. *Ibid.*
129. *Ibid.*
130. Sreenivasan, T.P (2017) *States in Indian diplomacy: when Sharjah ruler visited Kerala.* Available at: https://www.thehindu.com/opinion/lead/states-in-indian-diplomacy/article19803262.ece (Accessed: 9 April 2020)
131. Pant, Tewari. (2017) 'Para diplomacy and India: The growing role of states in Foreign policy', *LSE blog*, 12 January. Available at: https://blogs.lse.ac.uk/southasia/2017/01/12/paradiplomacy-and-india- the-growing-role-of-states-in-foreign-policy/ (Accessed: 13 April 2020)
132. *Ibid.*
133. *Ibid.*
134. *Ibid.*
135. Alvarez, M (2020) *The Rise of Para diplomacy in International Relations.* Available at: https://www.e-ir.info/2020/03/17/the-rise-of-paradiplomacy-in-international-relations/ (Accessed: 15 April 2020)
136. Miller, F (2022), U.S, *Supplement to Aristotle's Political Theory: Political Naturalism*, Stanford encyclopedia of philosophy, Stanford.
137. Hovet, T. (1963). United Nations Diplomacy. *Journal of International Affairs*, *17*(1), 29–41.
138. Kennedy, L., & Lucas, S. (2005). Enduring Freedom: Public Diplomacy and U.S. Foreign Policy. *American Quarterly*, *57*(2), 309–333.
139. Sarvjeet, S (2016), *Digital Diplomacy in India: Virtual networks, Real gains*, Master thesis, Universite Paris Sorbonne, viewed 15 April 2020, file:///Users/preethi/Downloads/MemoireSarvjeet%20SOODAN.pdf
140. Mazumdar, A. (2020). India's Public Diplomacy in the Twenty-First Century: Components, Objectives and Challenges. *India Quarterly, 76*, 24 - 39
141. *Ibid.*
142. Mazumdar, A. (2020). India's Public Diplomacy in the Twenty-First Century: Components, Objectives and Challenges. *India Quarterly, 76*, 24 - 39
143. *Ibid.*
144. *Ibid.*
145. Chang, Kim (2016) *The Myth of Soft Power in Asia.* Available at: https://www.e-ir.info/2016/05/24/the-myth-of-soft-power-in-asia/ (Accessed: 24 December 2020)

146. *Ibid.*
147. Vella, G (1998) Modern Diplomacy: Opening address. Available at: https://www.diplomacy.edu/resource/modern-diplomacy-opening-address/ (Accessed: 9 December 2019)
148. *Ibid.*
149. *Ibid.*
150. *Ibid.*
151. *Ibid.*
152. *Ibid.*
153. *Ibid.*
154. Javaid (2012) Public Diplomacy in Comparison to Traditional Diplomatic Approach, *Public Diplomacy.*
155. *Ibid.*
156. *Ibid.*
157. *Ibid.*
158. Mullen (2015) *India's soft power: Indian foreign policy*. London: Oxford university press.
159. Patkar, M (2017) India's Mediated Public Diplomacy on Social Media: Building Agendas and National Reputation in South Asia, PhD thesis, Scripps College of Communication of Ohio University, Athens, viewed 9 December 2019, https://etd.ohiolink.edu/apexprod/rws_etd/send_file/send?accession=ohiou151016626035757&disposition=inline
160. *Ibid.*
161. Mazumdar (2020) *India's Public Diplomacy in the Twenty-First Century: Components, Objectives and Challenges*. New Delhi: SAGE.
162. *Ibid.*
163. *Ibid.*
164. *Ibid.*
165. *Ibid.*
166. *Ibid.*
167. Hall, I (2012) India's New Public Diplomacy, *Asian Survey* (2012) 52 (6): 1089–1110. DOI: 10.1525/as.2012.52.6.1089.
168. *Ibid.*
169. Mazumdar (2020) *India's Public Diplomacy in the Twenty-First Century: Components, Objectives and Challenges*. New Delhi: SAGE.
170. *Ibid.*
171. *Ibid.*
172. *Ibid.*
173. Ritambhara. (2013) *On Indian Public Diplomacy*. Available at: https://www.e-ir.info/2013/04/30/on-Indian-public-diplomacy/ (Accessed: 9 November 2019)
174. *Ibid.*
175. *Ibid.*

176. *Ibid.*

177. *Ibid.*

178. Singh, S. (2018) Digital Diplomacy: India's Increasing Digital Footprint. 10.13140/RG.2.2.24554.44486.

179. *Ibid.*

180. *Ibid.*

181. *Ibid.*

182. *Ibid.*

183. *Ibid.*

184. Manor, I. (2017). The Digitalization of Diplomacy- Toward Clarification of a Fractured Terminology. *Digital Diplomacy Working Paper:* 10.13140/RG.2.2.31199.36004.

185. *Ibid.*

186. *Ibid.*

187. *Ibid.*

188. *Ibid.*

189. Hocking, Melissen (2015) *Diplomacy in the Digital Age.* Clingendael report, Netherlands Institute of International Relations. Available at: https://www.clingendael.org/sites/default/files/pdfs/Digital_Diplomacy_in_the_Digital%20Age_Clinge ndael_July2015.pdf

190. Amaresh, P (2020) *Digital Diplomacy: Connecting India with the World.* Available at: https://diplomatist.com/2020/05/21/digital-diplomacy-connecting-india-with-the-world/(Accessed: 9 February 2021)

191. Sharma (2017) Social Media as A Challenge to Traditional Indian Diplomacy: A Medium of Communication or A Mode of Diplomacy, *Jindal Journal of International Affairs*.

192. Engstrom, A (2019) *Digital Diplomacy: between promises and reality*, Master thesis, Utrecht University, Utrecht, viewed 17 November 2020, https://student-theses.uu.nl/bitstream/handle/20.500.12932/34391/FINAL_Master%20thesis_AlinaEngstrom.pdf?sequence=2

193. Chaudhury, R (2016) *India on top 10 ranking of global digital diplomacy: Diplomacy Live*, Available at: https://economictimes.indiatimes.com/news/politics-and-nation/india-on-top-10-ranking-of-global-digital-diplomacy-diplomacylive/articleshow/51715372.cms?utm_source=contentofinterest&utm_medium=text&utm_campaign=cp pst (Accessed: 29 November 2019)

194. Bagchi, I (2017) *MEA launches SAMEEP to take Indian foreign policy to students across the country.* Available at: https://timesofindia.indiatimes.com/india/mea-launches-sameep-to-take-indian-foreign-policy-to-students-across-the-country/articleshow/62139880.cms. (Accessed: 12 December 2020)

195. Palit. (2018) India's Use of Social Media in Public Diplomacy, Volume 3, Issue 3, *Public Diplomacy of Rising and Regional Powers*, Dec. 2018, pp. 151-171.

196. *Ibid.*

197. *Ibid.*

198. *Latest Twiplomacy study reveals 97% of all governments are on Twitter (10 July 2018).* Available at: https://www.bizcommunity.com/Article/1/669/179302.html (Accessed: 12 December 2020)

199. *Ibid.*

200. *Ibid.*

201. Adesina, O. (2017). Foreign policy in an era of digital diplomacy. *Cogent Social Sciences*. 19.169-189. 10.1080/23311886.2017.1297175.

202. Ebert, et.al. (2020). Cyber Resilience and Diplomacy in India. *EU cyber direct.* DOI: 10.13140/RG.2.2.18187.52004.

203. Digital ranking (2019) *Softpower30*. Available at: https://softpower30.com/ (Accessed: 2 September 2020)

204. Hedling, Bremberg (2021), Practice Approaches to the Digital Transformations of Diplomacy: Toward a New Research Agenda, *International Studies Review*, Volume 23, Issue 4, Pages 1595–1618, DOI: 10.1093/isr/viab027

205. Scott-Smith, Giles. (2018). Cultural Diplomacy. 10.4324/9780429493799-12.

206. Einbinder, M (2013) *Cultural Diplomacy Harmonizing International Relations through Music*, Master thesis, New York university, viewed 8 November 2019, https://www.culturaldiplomacy.org/pdf/case-studies/Cultural_Diplomacy_Harmonizing_International_Relations_through_Music_Mary_Einbinder.pdf

207. *Ibid.*

208. Amaresh, P (2020) *The Ramayana Diplomacy: Enhancing the Soft Power of India*. Available at: https://diplomatist.com/2020/11/11/the-ramayana-diplomacy-enhancing-the-soft-power-of-india/(Accessed: 21 December 2020)

209. *Ibid.*

210. *Ibid.*

211. *Ibid.*

212. *Ibid.*

213. *Ibid.*

214. *Ibid.*

215. *Ibid.*

216. *Ibid.*

217. *Ibid.*

218. Singh, Srivastava. (2014) 'Yoga as Indian soft power', *CPD blog*, 19 December, USC center for public diplomacy. Available at: https://uscpublicdiplomacy.org/blog/yoga-indian-soft-power.

219. Roche, E (2021) *Foreign ministry to promote yoga for well-being in show of soft power.* Available at: https://www.livemint.com/news/foreign-ministry-asks-to-embrace-yoga-to-battle-after-effects-of-covid-11624178206377.html (Accessed: 23 December 2021)

220. *Global soft power index* (2021). Available at: https://brandirectory.com/soft-power/ (Accessed: 9 January 2022)

221. *Ibid.*

222. *Ibid.*

223. *Ibid.*

Chapter Three

The State and Civil Society Interaction-Enhancing Soft Power of India

3.1. Introduction

Civil society is considered a society directed by people themselves and has its inception in classical occasions although the perception and interest have evolved and changed over duration of time. The Roman word "Societas Civilis" was the root concept of it holding a synonymy with a vigorous community. It is a cooperation of those social institutions of people who enjoy the distance and severance from the state and are independent; they push and influence the state administration on the support of their people whom they represent[1]. CSOs have presently attained notability due to their characteristics of being adaptable, cost-effective, non-bureaucratic, participatory and non-official and also of their capacity to influence the people untouched by the state[2]. Civil society points to those agencies, movements, institutions, cultural forces and social connections, which are both privately and voluntarily, established and which are not directly regulated by the state[3]. Italian politician, Gramsci found civil society in the political structure and saw it as a means of bourgeoisie hegemony. Rather than assuming it as a predicament, Gramsci saw civil society as the site for problem- solving[4]. German philosopher, Hegel was the chief philosopher to separate civil society and the state and several other scholars followed this[5].

World Bank describes Civil Society as which includes: "the wide array of NGOs and not for profit organizations that have a presence in public life, expressing the interests and values of their members or others, based on ethical, cultural, political, scientific, religious or philanthropic considerations"[6]. CSOs have arisen as a dominant force in global development in the last three decades[7]. The World Bank Group has been striving to reinforce its commitment to civil society since 1981 when the World Bank's Board of Directors adopted its initial operational strategy note on associations with CSOs[8].

This chapter begins by examining the role of non-state actors such as the CSOs. The chapter later progresses with the role of civil society and its interaction with the Indian state and the IOs also, highlighting civil society in the era of globalization. The chapter also focuses on the role of civil society in Indian media, Indian diplomacy and further bringing out the role of Indian civil society in the post-COVID era.

3.2 Civil Society

In the contemporary era, CSOs have come to enjoy political, intellectual and administrative influence[9]. The notion has been in continuation for a lengthy period[10]. Traditionally, CSOs and state have been used reciprocally and used as synonyms[11]. Today, a nation therefore needs civil societies to protect the basic human requirements against the austerity of the state. The rights of the depressed class, minority along with personal rights of liberty and freedom are preserved appropriately by civil society. The increasing power of Western states and global institutions emerges as the influence of standards or the impact of international civil society as raising the human rights discourse above authority has been viewed to be an evolved one that questions states and sets on a renewed and optimistic agenda[12]. Global governance, which is about norms and power and Ideas, culture and material forces further constitute it and it also helps generate norms, ideas and culture[13]. Global governance involves states and non-state actors, and it impacts life from the regional to the international levels.

It is a fact that non-state actors such as CSOs, cultural organizations and the private sector, today add to the soft power of the state.[14] The global engagement of such organizations often affects the way states are seen by other individuals and states, affecting events for mutual relations on matters related to trade, security etc.[15] This conceivably reinforces the claim for such organizations to play a more extensive part in global decision-making, as they are oftentimes ready to present first-hand insight on the grassroots suggestions of foreign policy[16]. Countries across the world should be more aware to work with organizations, groups and civil society in other countries apart from engaging with the diplomats of other nations[17]. More and more global engagement with important soft power and economic implications today is being seen at people-to-people, organization-to-organization and city-to-city level[18].

Traditional supra-national institutions where IR has taken place such as the U.N were designed for state-to-state negotiations. However, though non-state actors increasingly have an international voice through social media, they have had little ability to be involved in formal diplomatic processes. Therefore, as a result, ad-hoc solutions involving a variety of non-state actors are on the surge, which could be an important opportunity[19]. As the global community attempts to engage with enormous multifaceted global hurdles, the mounting power of non-state players could be an extraordinary occasion[20].

Presently, models of globalization have questioned the exclusivity of states as players in foreign affairs. Globalization connects far-flung societies and opens up areas for distinct social players[21]. The bearing of CSOs in IR has become frequently associated. They have performed a task in agenda framework, global diplomacy and law making[22]. IR cannot be wholly achieved without taking into account the efforts of CSOs[23]. In several western countries, the overall role of the state in government affairs was diminished [24]. In this setting, CSOs were able to subcontract several functions from the state and take up different positions as service providers[25]. CSOs have used their support at the global level to deliver notable results by establishing transnational channels[26].

Civil society development at the global level is predominantly centered on strengthening political structures with embedded democratic responsibility[27]. For instance, the European Union (EU) has followed a similar strategy by combining diverse CSOs in its governance tools[28]. IOs such as the SCO, BRICS etc. should likewise consider including CSOs just like how the U.N and EU have been utilizing CSOs at the global platform. CSOs have directed to enhance their entree to global decision-making, monitoring, agenda setting and implementation concerning international problems [29]. At one height there are CSOs instituted by states and IOs and at another, one notices CSOs that are viewed as criminals like the mafia and terrorist organizations. These shape the two extremes of amalgamation and exclusion[30]. Nonetheless, Civil society is distinct from the state, which indicates a ground where people can apprehend their self-interest, strengthen their self and discover the value of group development by relying on others for their welfare. It provides the people to engage in state functioning and consequently, it presents a substantial groundwork of citizenship. Though it is an aspect of the contemporary state and is subservient to its control, yet it is independent and freely created[31].

The role of civil society in government has become essential to ensure transparent and effective governance[32]. There is a deep need to construct a SMART (simple, moral, accountable, responsive and transparent) government to achieve the objective of good governance[33]. Notably, the role of CSOs in IR has become greatly relevant as they played a function in plan strategy, diplomacy and international law making[34]. Hence, IR cannot be thoroughly captured without taking into consideration the actions of CSOs[35]. CSOs have used their power at the international level to achieve effective results by building international networks[36]. The purpose of civil society in several global matters is to contribute to the normative conflict age of global public opinion[37].

Through the establishment of global promotion networks, and intimate co-operation with sensitive states and intergovernmental bodies, CSOs are molding the development of humanitarian standards in the contemporary era[38]. Civil society 'network diplomacy' is multidimensional as it includes many actors and the use of various tools and procedures[39]. Civil society channels are performing a more elevated role in disarmament diplomacy by forming the outcomes and effectiveness of mediation means. These CSOs are most productive in coordinating with mediation methods when they form sturdy partnerships with compatible states by thoroughly managing knowledge progress, and use unified and targeted support and campaign movements[40]. Civil society groups also perform a vital role to continually settle across ethnic frontiers for conflict resolution. For CSOs to be more active in peace building, they must be socially blended and promote synergy with other elements and stakeholders[41]. While economic advancement is imperative for survival and well being it is neither a panacea nor a substitute for the social difficulties that challenge us. Kofi Annan, former U.N secretary-general stated that, 'We must understand that well-built communities are created on three pillars which are security, growth and respect for human rights and the rule of law'[42]. Social innovation gets associated with the levels of freedom, peace, steadiness and security prevailing in a community. Justice, equality, empowerment and social justice compose the central values of righteous and democratic societies[43]. Therefore, state and civil society should indeed interact well and promote enhanced association for the welfare of the communities in a nation.

3.3 Civil Society in India

India is a nation that has an ancient past, an active today and an enthusiastic tomorrow[44]. The notion of a new India in the future is being shown by the present government with a desire for a more flourishing economy, suitable living standards, robust defence establishment, peaceful community in the times to come[45]. It is observed that the government implements many schemes and puts forward the budget, awareness drives and advertisements to accomplish the aspiration of new India. Nevertheless, this seems to be inept in building a more innovative and unique story of India due to the inability of active diplomatic cooperation of the CSOs with the government and its enhanced participation. A CSO is a necessity in a progressive democracy like India and for developing such values and norms; the purpose conducted by civil society is imperative. More comprehensive interests of the people, common civic outcomes can solely be accomplished through the actuality of a throbbing civil society[46]. However, in nations like the U.S, civil societies are well instituted, while in emerging nations like India, it is nevertheless under-developed.

People in a civil society voluntarily come forward collectively to accomplish the coveted purpose of the well being of the community or to support the difficulties of people before the country where the lacuna of the country can be well furnished by the CSOs. India in this context requires an active collaboration of civil society in the building of a "New India". Likewise, for all the new initiatives, schemes that impact a nation and also its diplomacy with other nations, the state requires the cooperation and knowledge of the community and its citizens and there is no more reliable organization than the civil society to realize this goal. For instance, the engagement of civil society in the "Incredible India campaign" had an immense progress in bringing out a transformation in the society to an extent[47].

India has been a civilized nation with a vibrant cultural legacy. However, western values penetrated this Indian society with the coming of the British. A struggle between traditional values and modernity existed. Though many people aimlessly grasped the contemporary life of the west, many social reformers wanted to enhance the Hindu culture making it fit the contemporary period. Western values of individualism, open-mindedness and constitutionalism made their encroachment into Indian society that led to political consciousness. British hegemonic rule economically impoverished India and halted the growing Indian nationalism with the strategy of 'divide and rule.' The roots of communalism intruded into the nation leading to post-independent India. Later, the new ruling class desired to make the country flourishing at par with other advanced countries of the world, post-independence. India is a more externally involved nation twenty years after it started to deregulate its economy. Due to this, the society wanted to preserve their interest through engagements and cooperation. In this way, the Indian civil society became more proficient with civic values and likewise acquired the inclination to establish itself autonomous of state authority where personal liberties and rights are safeguarded and several independent organizations were formed within the state. A long-isolated country and society are increasing the description of what compounds foreign ties. Much of this development is stimulated by sources of strength on the diplomatic institution of India, which are a sound diaspora, an energetic business community and a boisterous and dynamic news media. The assistance of Indian citizens abroad and the Indian capital is now a legitimate expectation of the country's diplomacy.

The beginning of the 20th century witnessed significant change of spontaneous movements in India. Some people supported the contemporary life of the occidental evangelists and social reformers like Raja Ram Mohan Roy, Dayananda and Vivekananda who aspired to transform the Hindu customs and traditions to shape it to make it fitting to the modern era. These social reforms sparked the attention and need for fundamental rights and violation that drove to great disagreement towards the British colonial rule. The struggle for independence phase marked the advent of Mahatma Gandhi where voluntary action brought on a completely brand-new purpose. Gandhi's direction to gather the crowds into simple as well as powerful rallies and demonstrations brought to the platform of civil society sensational movements such as Satyagraha, civil disobedience and non-cooperation. During the late 1970s and 1980s, the Emergency crisis in India further led the footing for the emergence of diverse protest campaigns and a renaissance of CSOs. Indian political scientists analyzing the development of the civil society and state have perceived significant differences between this growth in India and related developments in the occidental nations. The democratic character of the civil society of India is exhibited in the establishment of a democratic republic accompanying the enactment of a democratic constitution. 'Good governance', is the productive implementation of judgments and policies and civil society is the most suitable forum to administer public engagement. Possessing closeness to the Indian people, civil society can, therefore, be the medium for administering methods and policies anchored by the executive hence addressing good governance as an actuality.

The inceptions of modern Indian civil society can be ascertained to the initial times of the 20th centenary and the evolution of the Indian National Congress (INC). The new ruling class, after India's independence, aspired to build a prosperous India on par with other advanced countries of the world. Following the independence struggle, the country established a

Planning Commission that put forth the five-year plans for India's economic and political progress. The creation of Self Help Groups (SHGs), National Rural Livelihoods Mission (NRLM), ASHA workers, Implementation of the National Rural Employment Guarantee (NREGA) Act, and many more major programmes present the interaction of civil society and the Government of India. The National Advisory Council (NAC) of India is a body of specialists from civil society under the Prime Minister Office (PMO) that does the job of crucial review and skilled or expert advisory. India's civil society has been astoundingly efficient in leading concerns to the vanguard of Indian society. The democratic character of the Indian civil society is displayed in the establishment of a democratic state simultaneously with the enactment of a democratic polity. The amicable co-existence of both the civil society and the state preserves the interest of both the citizens and the state. At times, there is a particular emergence of disagreement between the state and the civil society, as the requirements and expectation of the community are not achieved. Seldom, the state likewise neglects the importance of the majority and meddles in the field of civil society. A welfare state like India is required to guarantee social rights along with economic growth. Various schemes are adopted for the elimination of illiteracy, poverty, unemployment, malnutrition and so on.

In the modern times, more emphasis has been given to decentralization of authority, participation of the community in the method of administration and guaranteeing clarity in government functioning with the Right to Information (RTI). Through the development of state functions, excessive bureaucratization became the establishment of the system through crony capitalism, corruption, nepotism, red-tapism etc. Due to this, the Indian civil society has raised its call against such a development. Also, the regional incongruity in economic growth and constant neglect of several grievances point to the rise of criminalization of politics, communalism, and terrorism, casteism that are perils to civil society. Concerning the recent amendment of the Foreign Currency Regulation Act (FCRA), 2010, many CSOs have begun to question these amendments, particularly at a point when India needs sturdy CSOs and channels to deal with a variety of difficulties including the deleterious outcomes of the Covid-19 pandemic. Consequently, given the position of NGOs in the growing sector of the country, there is a necessity to balance between the states immediate and the independence of NGOs and to put a restraint on NGOs that are involved in unlawful pursuits.

3.4 The Synergy between Indian State and Its Civil Society

India has millions of CSOs that include diaspora groups, NGOs, social movements, labor organizations, academia, think tanks, charitable institutions etc. operating in a diversity of fields. The national resistance movement, initiated by the INC became the principal beginning of the civil society movement in early 20th century British India. The view of the state officials through the emergency in India (1975-1977) presented a noteworthy reason for the civil society to be expressive and boisterous[48]. Today, civil society in the country is a developing trend that is grabbing impulse due to a swelling amount of CSOs. India's present-day civil society has been considered effective in fields working for a broad variety of matters[49]. The agenda of civil society changed over the times from fighting to build democracy to protecting it. "Good governance" is the productive implementation of policies and decisions where civil society is the most desirable forum to direct public engagement[50]. India is considered one of the few nations to have never been directed to military or autocratic governments. If the national emergency is considered as the one point it came nearest to such a rule, the powerful opposition and influence by the Indian civil society upon the curbing of fundamental rights symbolize a robust civil society with high-powered leaders.

The Hindu notion of Dharma as well as other religions in India laid weight on the moralistic code of behavior and conduct that sequentially helps the common good of the nation. In the country, with regard to religion and ahead, we observe the vibrant civil society advances that have promoted community and have attempted to bring back state behavior to the ethical sphere[51]. The primary drive to create a civil liberties organization was first steered by Jawaharlal Nehru in 1936 when he established the Indian Civil Liberties union (ICLU) with Rabindranath Tagore as its president. The responsibility of the nation is to preserve these freedoms[52]. Discussions in India over civil rights have advanced into more extensive areas of democratic rights and then to individual rights. Besides new dimensions have developed as cultural movements concentrating on women, regional, minority and environmental problems evolved into locus. In India, every citizen is a recipient of the rights given by the constitution of the country and has the responsibility of shoving the duties originating from it. The commitments of the Republic of India towards its people have been pronounced in the constitution especially in the segments on Fundamental Rights and Directive Principles of State Policy (DPSP)[53]. It is acknowledged now that a liberal, equitable and civilized society respects basic human rights not just of its nationals but all communities, has a state factor that is clear in its functioning and promotes the growth of a robust civil society. CSOs help in bridging gaps in the government programmes, play the role of an enabler through SHGs and community-level outfits, act as important pressure groups through political NGOs to put pressure on public policy and educate the public and further act as a social mediator concerning the social situation in accomplishing aspired outcomes of change in the community. They have played a significant role in participative governance through many initiatives that have contributed to some of the path-breaking laws in India such as RTI, the Right to Education (RTE) act 2009 and Forest Rights Act 2006.

The policymaking approach in the country from the Independence till the 1980s focused around the "State" as the creator of policy, with restricted participation from non-state players. The state attempted to solve societal quandaries by choosing a top-down, systematic strategy to policymaking by depending on its organizations to accomplish this function. It was during this time that through the Planning Commission significant institutional developments in the scientific or technocratic means of policymaking were built. Later, with the start of liberalization and globalization, the role of the state shifted to a complex position and there was considerably higher scrutiny of public policy from the foundation. This focus led to issues of suitable arrangements, procedures and methods for policy formulation.

Attention shifted to questions of appropriate policies and structures, processes for policy formulation, developing the ability of policymakers and assessing policy ends. Opening up of policymaking to non-State players required re-conceptualization of governance from a centralized, top-down conventional form of 'government' to a further collaborative, horizontal composition and a non-hierarchical framework that had to be forthwith based on lobbying, networking and mediation. The transformation from 'government' to 'governance as a network' performed a vital purpose in opening up policymaking to organizations, influences from non-State players, including the impact of international establishments. The state of perplexity has been the symbol of state-civil society relations in the country where the State has mounted and civil society endured at the edges. Nevertheless, a few establishments like the National Advisory Council (NAC) set up by the UPA government in 2004 helped in facilitating government-civil society networking[54]. The NAC has likewise performed a crucial function in bringing in enactment like the MNREGA, RTI etc. Frequently, there is a noticeable transformation in the State's strategy to formally include civil society players in policy channels. As CSOs start to involve actively in policymaking, on part of citizens and marginalized societies, they are frequently being called on by the state, and different stakeholders like academics, media and segments of citizens.

Indians, as informed citizens cannot desire good governance without civil society's commitment. A well-functioning government requires people's cooperation and investment. The socio-economic predicaments tormenting our country are enormous and require paramount consideration. India is also required to improve its human development rank, being at the bottom. Despite the presence of diverse NGOs that concentrate on several societal causes, the NGOs in India have been paid less attention to the broader problem of clefts in governance and policymaking shortfalls. Several quandaries the country faces now are an outcome of systemic predicaments and fixing them should be an uppermost preference[55]. Lately, the problem of women's empowerment in India has attained influence. State and civil society has undertaken matters such as dwindling sex ratio, huge school dropouts, inadequate access to education, scarcity of healthcare etc. India requires skilled people, fresh approaches and technology despite having the tools and sources to achieve multi-dimensional planned projects. The sustainability and range of transformation can solely be accomplished with state and civil society engagement though working with the state can sometimes be challenging. However, without engaging with the state, the civil society establishments cannot look forward to long-term sustained development. One observes how the NGOs in the country have attempted to supersede the state and have been incapable to surmount or sustain their influence. Good governance shapes the pleasant setting for overall economic advancement and expansion. Globally also only some institutions have taken great influence actions in this respect and are confidently interlacing with the government. There is a need to enhance human capital to produce future leaders to hope for a change in governance. There is a call for more numerous NGOs to function in raising capability in the state, to promote its purpose more productively and effectively[56].

The occupation of various cultural and linguistic groups in India has led to ethnic pluralism where each ethnic organization has been explaining its interests in words of the protection of its distinct uniqueness[57]. In the northeast, an essential yet neglected part of India civil society has risen continuously over the last few decades. CSOs especially youth and student organizations have increased on the rims of the country's political system, in the buffer area between radical organizations and political parties[58]. The country's northeast region has its constraints and opportunities, weaknesses and strengths and requirements and preferences, but the growth initiatives so far have followed the national panoramas of growth and the area remains to be backward notwithstanding some exclusive schemes, programmes and establishments such as the North Eastern Council (NEC) and Development of the North Eastern Region (DONER)[59].

In an active and sound democracy like India, there is no remorse in accepting the shortcomings and the gaps that subsist in the policies and organizations about human rights[60]. In this context education in human rights culture becomes critically relevant in educational establishments. Also, few CSOs encounter constraints because they engage with global human rights mechanisms and stress the human rights and civil society conditions in India where these CSOs have witnessed their capacity to get funding from global sources are being curbed.[61] Though article 19 of the Indian constitution ensures all citizens the right to form associations, in contemporary times the state has frequently used a string of stratagems to target CSOs and halt their pursuits[62]. The aforementioned challenging setting produced by limitations and attacks on CSOs, journalists and human rights supporters has prompted many to self-censor[63]. CSOs must accordingly take a position in aiding us to meet the moral hurdles of our today.

However, issues are emanating from CSOs such as lack of transparency and accountability where many CSOs are being blacklisted, lack of credibility and weakening development activities incase of Greenpeace, Amnesty etc. that decreased the country's GDP by 2-3% annually as per the reports of India's Intelligence Bureau (IB)[64]. It is crucial for CSOs to accomplish and maintain a high degree of transparency concerning not just the funds but also how they perform. They need to keep their expenditure and income open to public analysis. Also, Indian federalism is gravely imperiled by populist imperatives arising in the states, which infringe so considerably into the country's administration as to enfeeble government and the union executive. The establishment of the state finance commission has also not been equipped enough to accomplish fiscal devolution to the local administration and realize a more inclusive and powerful decentralized governance in India[65].

In the last two decades, civil society in India has shown significant response to the economic, social and political quandaries and has been able to shape policies, demanded responsibility and further built cultural harmony in the wake of fundamentalism and communalism in India. An Indian Express report states that civil society has presently thoroughly permeated our daily discourse due to Anna Hazare[66]. According to former finance minister late Arun Jaitley, "In any developing society and any mature society, there will be a role for civil society"[67]. The Indian constitutional interpretation of the rule of law connects its four core understandings such as development, governance, rights and justice. Political scientists, lawyers, social philosophers, courts of law, state personalities and activists, civil society groups and educated citizens have been enthusiastic participants[68].

Furthermore, author Sunil Khilnani has described 'layered Indianess' that explicitly identified linguistic and social identities. This was displayed in the end product – a union of states, represented by Ivor Jennings as 'a federation with robust centralizing tendencies[69]. Enhanced need for commodity stocks obtained from mining, Speedy economic growth, resilient commodity markets, underdevelopment and poverty in mineral resource-rich states have presented the backdrop for a discussion on 'resource federalism' in India. The Indian constitution has had to face questions about the performance of its federal setting in the context of resource growth, protection of human, legal and fundamental rights; the steadiness between political coordination; local environmental and social responsibilities, economic and developmental administration. A 2010 report of the committee on center-state ties piously declares that 'cooperative federalism' is the solution in which 'diplomacy or statecraft would lead to politics'[70].

In the last decade, the discussion on democratization in the third world has been greatly shaped by theories highlighting the value of an autonomous civil society[71]. Civil society is a very comprehensive notion and cannot be bound to just some organizations whose actions are obvious and consequently can be examined. It is a concept that is inclusive of a meaning of the socio-political and economic life. Therefore there are divergences of opinion within the civil society of the advanced and that of the developing nations all though, there is differences in the civil society of the developing nations as well [72]. Every third-world nation and every democracy has its unique form of state-civil society association, and almost all states have had a colonial past that shaped these relations[73]. Civil society should therefore have a base in a full-fledged democracy and a thoughtful state society[74].

Chandhoke notes that civil society cannot do without the state. Therefore civil society is a critique of the state but is not anti-state. It can neither be a replacement for the state as it nevertheless lacks the method, organization and exactness of the state. (Chandhoke, Neera, n. 71, p 30.) 'Civil Society' is also not only as a renovated or resurgent agenda formed by social and political scientists but is a contemporary debate about an idealized society (Bottomore: 1993, J. Arato and J.C. Alexander: 2001, Krishnan Kumar: 1993/97). As the state is frequently viewed as ineffective and corrupt, the NGOs are described as active and responsible. However, leaving the negative portrayal of the state away, the concrete representation of civil society rests more on a theoretical and ideological interpretation rather than an authentic appraisal of civil society in India presently[75]. The role of states and civil society is also molding and promoting corporate social responsibility (CSR) in India today.

Concerning agriculture and the environment, there are several hurdles that CSOs must face to discuss long-term citizen movement on agriculture and trade problems in India[76]. There are diverse CSOs operating for the security of agriculture, biodiversity and nature, which are regarded vital for a strong and clean sound image of India on the global stage. The past civil society campaigns like the "Chipko", "Appiko" movements for the protection of nature to the contemporary time "Narmada Bachao Abhiyan" and "Aravali Bachao" have attempted to accomplish a similar purpose in synergy with the notion of new India. Since the last two decades, plenty of NGOs in India have been operating in the domain of environmental safeguard. The CSOs views must be taken into consideration by the government. For instance, regarding the farmer suicides in the Vidarbha region, members of civil society Vidarbha Jan Andolan Samiti (VJAS) and Vidarbha Civil Society Collective conclude that their views and recommendations have not been taken into account the implementation of major bills such as the Resettlement and Rehabilitation Bill 2011 and the National Land Acquisition. The recent farm bills have likewise created a discord between the state and CSOs. However, the Poorest Areas Civil Society (PACS) program in the agricultural domain contributed to further establish and achieve the Mahatma Gandhi Employment Guarantee Act (NREGA) scheme greatly to serve all the targeted districts (PACS, 2007)[77]. Furthermore, in the energy sector, there has been enhanced energy diplomacy cooperation of India with other nations through various renewable energy projects and also the establishment of International Solar Alliance (ISA) that is considered a game changer[78].

With regard to women's empowerment, several Indian CSOs (women's organizations) have been included in the governmental progress plans. Some of the well-known NGOs include Sewa, Snehalaya, Azad Foundation, Crea, Vimochana etc.[79] As women constitute half of the country's population, without their cooperation and participation, equitable and sustainable progress is unlikely. The purpose of NGOs towards the empowerment of women is extremely essential in the Indian situation, as their participation in the advancement of the nation becomes a hurdle. The issue of women empowerment among CSOs has gradually increased in India considering the time the 1975 global gathering opened the "U.N Decade for Women"[80]. It is crucial to form women's access to resources and render handholding when they take up entrepreneurial pursuits[81]. SHGs and NHGs (Neighborhood Groups) have also been playing an enhanced role in empowering women[82]. The five-year government plans established in India have likewise played a high role in women empowerment. Hence, it is critical to discuss women's issues and involve them in the growth process that is one of the major contributions of CSOs[83].

In the education domain, universal education has been the agenda for the Indian government's development agenda following the 1950s[84]. The Universal Declaration of Human Rights (UDHR) declares that education is a human right and most nations have committed to ensuring the right to universal, free and compulsory education, through the ratification of at least the United Nations Convention on the Rights of the Child (UNCRC)[85]. In this context, the GOI should educate the children has implemented numerous schemes since several decades. Solely those who have sufficient money to educate themselves can enjoy education in the country. Due to this situation, the poor lack the resources and are not capable to adopt any other means of living, apart from work that requires hand-operated labor[86]. Unfortunately, presently there exists a large gap within the nations global legal responsibilities to grant universal free and quality education and the actuality of guaranteeing such quality education for all where the civil society performs a vital task[87]. There exists social, ethnic, linguistic, gender discrimination and also discrimination among the disabled children who are forced to work. CSOs act as more confidential with communities and can be a bridge where the teacher, student or parent's concerns about the state of education services influence the policymakers[88]. They collectively can also assist to influence the national education policies closer to attaining the aim of accomplishing the right to education for all and not omitting any child or adolescent behind.[89] CSOs have also participated in policy dialogues for the implementation of education policies in the past[90]. Well known CSOs such as the Akshaya Patra Foundation (TAPF), Teach for India (TFI), Make A Difference (MAD) etc., have furthermore played a great role in initiating the drive for literacy and providing mid-day meals in schools. As philosopher Aristotle quoted, "The roots of education are bitter, but the fruit is sweet", the Indian education system must act now to evolve for the better in the coming years that gives the students equal opportunities to shine better for tomorrow.

According to United Nations Population Fund (UNFPA), India has its largest ever adolescent and youth population. India will advance to have one of the youngest populations in the world by 2030. The country is undergoing a demographic pane of opportunity, a "youth bulge" that will remain till 2025. The Economic Survey 2019 has mentioned regarding the additional jobs to maintain with the proposed yearly increases in the working-age group[91]. Therefore, India needs a workforce that is well educated and trained besides being suitably skilled[92]. As the country strives to become a knowledge economy, the young population is being left behind. India that aspires to become a $5 trillion economy by 2024-25 should in every respect include the young population to make the country advance in the right direction. With this, the proper association between the state and civil society is crucial and their role is pivotal in the country's progress.

3.5 The Indian Media and Civil Society

Media is considered the fourth pillar of Indian democracy and free media has a pivotal purpose in enhancing Indian diplomacy to promote India's soft power. CSOs can serve to counteract the influence of the state, fight authoritarianism and assure that the state is not regulated by vested interests[93]. The media can act as a watchdog by unveiling corruption and can accommodate to strengthen accountability and good governance by presenting authentic, fair and appropriate data that is of importance and pertinence to the society[94]. Indian economist, Amartya Sen noted that it is not tough to see why free, dynamic and active media can support the needed long-winded process significantly. The media as per Sen is critical not just for democracy but for the pursuance of justice in general[95]. Indian public diplomacy makes an effort to pat into the gaits made by non-state actors to expand its power, but the latter's movements are not always complimentary. For instance, American Sikhs who is a section of the Indian diaspora were unhappy with India following "Operation Blue Star", an Indian army onslaught against the Golden Temple in 1984. In the before-mentioned circumstances, non-state actors may impair certain efforts. So much depends on circumstances, as circumstances determine the interaction between state and non-state players in the matter of PD.

Media in India first came into existence in 1780 with the opening of the first newspaper named 'The Bengal Gazette' and thereafter which it has continued to evolve[96]. Since then media in India has been performing a highly important function in forming individual perceptions and beliefs. For a democratic nation, the learning path is imperative; freedom to understand or communicate is a crucial component to unfold and expose the fact, to secure self-fulfillment and self-development of people and to further guarantee the cooperation of the citizens in a democracy[97]. While India was on the way to be an independent nation, Indian leader, Mahatma Gandhi was a great mass communicator who left out no means, no way to awaken the mindfulness of the public and infuse into the people the imperative of their effective cooperation in the journey. Presently, nearly every, journalism as it survives developed out of citizen journalism in India[98]. The notion of citizen journalism has amassed mediums such as journals, television, newspapers, the radio and the Internet[99]. So, besides the Internet, no other tool grants total freedom of expression to the citizens[100]. The part that the media can play, as a medium, to lessen friction is necessary. Media further promotes civil society in its attempts at conflict resolution. Social media further expedites some civil society moves too. The worldwide society has identified the position of the media in a post-conflict community and its value[101]. A credible news media empowers well-informed citizen decision-making that is freely used, indeed, has contributed to democratization. Engagement in the media's part in maintaining peace and democratic transformation advances to expand. Good journalism is a continuous means of exploring solutions[102]. By supporting initiatives and schemes like the "Incredible India" etc., the media has been considerably prosperous in developing social values and preserving the environment to some amount. Free media has also performed a very notable role in improving the voter's turnout. Media instantly can't shape the policy but unquestionably, it can criticize the policy and push the state to improve the policy if in any case, it is not in the interest of the citizens. The philosopher John Rawls has observed that considerably equal access to the media was to limit politics being taken by groups of individual economic control that will make it challenging for equitably responsible citizens to have equitable opportunities to mold politics, notwithstanding of their class[103]. Therefore, the role of media influences policy-making and consequently makes the state and its administrative system more democratic.

In the case of civil society in Internet governance, strong and comprehensive Internet governance must reflect the increasing significance of the Internet for international social, economic, and civic life. Several small and emerging nations in common and their civil societies, in specific, are not included in global digital means for a broad extent of purposes, including the need for expertise, resources, and institutional potential to nurture an impactful strategy bearing[104]. Internet governance matters reshape social, security, employment, political, economic, rule of law, and many more features of India's contemporary and prospective growth. In India, presently, they are not sufficiently engaged in forming strategies and decision-making on local, provincial, and international levels. The role of civil society in the digital domain hence is indispensable in terms of neo-realism and soft power for India and for the development Agenda 2030. Key advancements in modern diplomacy, in particular concerns how digital technologies affect the development of new characters, the shaping of the diplomatic plan, and moves in the geopolitical context[105]. Today, several global organizations, bilateral contributors and NGOs started to search for possibilities for media assistance programmes[106]. Several humanitarian countries such as Sweden, the United Kingdom, Switzerland, Netherlands, Denmark etc. have begun media assistance programmes in their global support policies. Likewise, significant organizations like the World Bank, Council of Europe and UNESCO have advanced considerably in media pursuits as a component of human rights and democratization agendas[107].

The non-state actor PD of India's active media scene is quite autonomous of state control and regularly quite decisive of the state. Popular English media TV channels such as CNN-IBN, Times Now etc. as well as other regional language channels perform a vital part in acquainting international and national public. In the various terrorist attacks such as the 2008 Mumbai terrorist attacks, Uri attacks etc. these channels performed an important role through live telecast by communicating to the world about the terrorists. However, extreme coverage or promotion of sensitive news has been directed to communal tumults. For instance, the 1984 Sikh Riots and the 2002 Gujarat Riots. The coverage by the media on such incidents has gained strong criticisms[108]. Continuous repetition of the news, particularly sensational news, produces indifference and insensitivity. The Media is deemed to be a two sides weapon[109]. Both media and civil society while playing an essential role have their boundaries and are likewise seldom reprimanded for their one-sided or negative character. In the last few years, the Indian media has been subjected to criticism and scrutiny for ignoring its commitments to social engagement. Precarious commercial practices in media have altered the framework of Indian constitutionalism. Corporates get the most advantage if they can be proximate to the agent lobby of power. With the rise of a target rating point (TRP) and paid news environment the recent years, the trust over the media is gradually diminishing through odious acts of taking cash from the corporate organizations, state, ideological associations or large associations. "Power corrupts and absolute power corrupts even more[110]". Therefore, several news media channels have begun selective reporting. A responsible media is a necessity to elevate the nation to maxima by rendering firm backing for its growth and unaccountable media can create confusion in the community[111]. In this context, the Indian Media today is not being regarded as neutral and is seen taking sides and depending on the political party they are with where the message they take to the society is further changed.

Media is a reflector of society and a mighty tool in implementing laws. The freedom of the press in India is a boon for society. Nevertheless, this boon can go awry when manipulation occurs. Citizen-friendly democracy is a hope that the media should endeavor for in a nation like India. In any democracy, the diminishing of pillars is ever more impairing. The people need to reach the central trunk, to clip the faulty aerial roots that are growing and destroying society[112]. The great Martin Luther King Jr. stated, "The ultimate measure of a man is not where he stands in moments of comfort and convenience, but where he stands at a time of challenge and controversy"[113]. In this context, accordingly, though the data protection bill as recommended by B.N.Srikrishna Committee would check the spreading of fake news and misinformation on the media, in contemporary challenging times fractured by discord and fallacious information, to defend the pillars of democracy will require tolerance and understanding. Therefore, it is important for all three pillars of Indian democracy to balance well for a stable functioning of the civil society.

3.6 Enhancing India's Diplomacy through Civil Society

Inter-state relations in the 20th century were formed through diplomacy focused on the head of the executive power[114]. Notwithstanding the liberal metamorphoses from the earlier centuries, diplomats held dressed with legitimacy that nevertheless lacked institutional solidity to be transferred to the people[115]. Foreign policy was drawn based on univocal national interest[116]. Diplomacy was based on privacy and decision-making centralization on the administrative authority was proved[117]. The increase of inter-regionalism has shown the development of a new area of governance, which is known as the "unofficial diplomacy" that involves several non-state actors who contribute to the description of the new global system.

In the contemporary era, non-state players have a sizable influence on the area of state diplomacy in a globalized world signalized by enhanced synergy among the public and CSOs across the world. Seldom, attempts by non-state players generate more productive outcomes than that of the state. The State later tends to touch into the energies of the non-state actors[118]. The dramatic enlargement of India's assistance programmes under the DPA within the MEA followed a fairly robust drive to the further popular aspects of multilateral and commercial economic diplomacy[119]. The public opinion provided through the discussion with CSOs has the potential to intensify the performance of the DPA that is presently represented by a tiny segment of the Indian civil society, often the educated groups[120]. Indian embassies have likewise actively involved in organizing trade shows and 'Make in India' events. Therefore, Indian diplomacy is no separate where numerous non-state players are strengthening India's attempts in an essential way. Nevertheless, the pattern of cooperation among state and non-state players, in the area of diplomacy is somewhat complicated and depends on the circumstances[121]. In the past, charismatic leaderships from Gandhi legacy to Nehru and its family have played a pivotal position in Indian state origin and widely dominated its decision-making, particularly concerning foreign policy[122]. Indian decision-making in the present era on foreign policy happens within this federalist, parliamentary, democratic and profoundly social diverse setting[123].

The further empowerment of civil society goes forward with the "track-two" diplomacy that indicates NGOs and informal communications among state and non-state players like scholars, social organizations and NGOs (Acharya, 2004)[124]. Nevertheless, the associates in "track-two" diplomacy have a particular relationship with state policymakers where the notion discussed in the informal context can display and seep into the thought of official policy gatherings (Kaye, 2005: 7)[125]. The civil society indigenous proactivity in India did not translate toward large mobilizations on foreign policy matters. The independence movement embraced the NAM, which was likewise adopted domestically by the people of India. In the initial five decades of the Indian state, there was a small room for transnational fight networks, or also for indigenous predicaments connected to the global sphere. Post-1991 liberalization led to addressing civil society demands to foreign policy decision-making. Trade organizations have also provided for efficiently intensifying some institutional defects in Indian diplomacy, particularly the CII and the FICCI[126]. The business sector will act closer to foreign policy decision-making in India considering the state is ineffective for improving diplomacy institutional defects[127]. Following the last two governments, public discussions with civil society generated where information and transparency networks have been formed. The likewise stimulus cannot be so well observed in Indian diplomacy that has developed more structured vicinity with the business sector that has operated for several occasions the part of diplomat advisors. The domestic dynamism of India was not changed into more comprehensive mobilizations on foreign policy[128].

However, the track level II diplomacy has been building strength in this manner. As state organizations crystallize their democratic government, accountability key channels and social examination over state actions may likewise reinforce and serve to become more prevalent and convenient (Robert Putnam-1988). State civil society has become an essential actor to pressurize and to necessitate decisions concerning state foreign actions. State civil society expands its scope for progress through a foreign policy that is further responsible in presence of its state institutions. Civil society channels are also performing a more prominent role in disarmament diplomacy, developing the dynamics and upshots of mediation methods. Civil society 'network diplomacy' is multidimensional which requires multiple players and the use of various tools and approaches[129]. For instance, the Indian-Americans have much weight on economic and strategic affairs where they performed a vital purpose in the dissolution of the sanctions forced on India following the 1998 nuclear testing and the signing of the Indo-U.S. Civil Nuclear Agreement. Also, CSOs act as an immeasurable route between the "State and the civil society" and India should consider magnifying "PD division" by involving CSOs to enhance the soft power of India in the years to come.

Moreover, in the last few years, likewise there has been an increase in various think tanks in the fields of politics, IR, social sciences, environment in India that have played a major role in enhancing government and civil society cooperation. Some of the prominent think tanks in India such as the Observer Research Foundation (ORF), Centre for Dialogue and Reconciliation (CDR), Centre for Land Warfare Studies (CLAWS), Indian Council of World Affairs (ICWA), Council On Energy, Environment and Water (CEEW), National Knowledge Commission (NKC), Vivekananda International Foundation (VIF) etc., have played a major role in enhancing India's soft power diplomacy through dialogues, conferences and publications. Despite this, there's a mismatch between India's natural strengths and its strategic focus where the country's strategic thinking is military-centric[130]. Today, many of the country's think tanks are dominated by armed forces. In this setting, though the opinions of the armed forces are important, India's think tanks should consider segregating the opinions of diplomats, academicians etc. and the military to avoid further confusion. The think tanks should be invested profoundly in experts and analysts who examine the political and economic situations of nations across the world, to understand how India can engage their interests. Also, (Markey, 2009) notes a string of checks for a successful Indian diplomacy action overseas directed at putting India in contemporary global challenges and on improving the country's regional leadership like the tiny size of Indian diplomatic channels, lack of information on state actions to be analyzed by autonomous, think tanks and well-equipped universities apart from the lack of interest of the private sector and the media to positively mesh in the discussions on international affairs.

Professor Mukund Dubey has determined that 'diplomacy works on a very thin edge of practical opportunities'. In India's case, the rim is granted by outsiders understanding of the nation's strengths and gaps. This observation depends also on what is occurring inside India than what is happening outside. Diplomacy has been hand-woven of this effort. Enduringly but persistently it has served to shape opinions, innovate solutions and link gaps[131]. To successfully administer foreign policy approach across nations, Indian diplomatic embassies must also consistently remain in touch with the social, political, economic certainties of the nation they work in. Likewise, the Indian embassies must also learn and bring out the ideas from the successful CSOs of Japan, Switzerland, Canada and Australia and their way of functioning to implement them in India. Indian diplomats will also require being in continuous touch with local CSOs at all levels. For robust cooperation between CSOs and diplomacy, the government should increase the staff in all levels at the MEA apart from increasing the number of Diplomats. Importantly, expanding the staff at the MEA through lateral entry and fellowships that could help in performing a vital role in Para-diplomacy, which in the process could involve both the regional governments and the CSOs to enhance India's diplomacy and soft power at the global level.

Furthermore, Indian diplomats need to interact with the civil society of the countries they are posted in rather than spending most of their working hours thinking solely about India. Indian embassies abroad in this way can create a positive impact, which could make the visits by the Indian Prime Minister or the Foreign Minister more flexible with the overseas governments. This could likewise help in designing a proper path and also heighten India's representation abroad. The GOI should consider foreign and diplomacy as a driving necessity and not a luxury. This driving need must occur in New Delhi, not merely in Indian embassies abroad. To strongly administer foreign policy approach across nations, Indian diplomatic embassies must also consistently remain in touch with the social, political, economic certainties of the nation they work in. With the Industrial Revolution 4.0, Artificial Intelligence (AI) and 5G as the contemporary constituents for the country's economic growth, India will have to retool its economic diplomacy. The establishment of the NEST [New, Emerging & Strategic Technologies] as a new department in the MEA is an appreciated initiative[132].

The World Economic Forum (WEF) report "The Future Role of Civil Society" further alludes to the attention of civil society leaders globally concerning means in which they can remain important and advance to influence global governance processes together (WEF, 2013, p.17) and in this view CSO responses to advancement, participation is vital[133]. Civil society has been identified presently as a major stakeholder in development associated with foreign policy matters, particularly civil society from middle-income nations and the 'rising powers' like India (Poskitt and Shankland, 2014; Shankland and Constantine, 2014). The Forum for Indian Development Cooperation (FIDC) is presently seen as a forum for policy discussion and dialogue within which civil society in India has been able to make vital participation (Moilwa, 2015, p.3). FIDC is also a forum for more inclusive synergy between the MEA and members of CSOs[134]. However, Civil society involvement has been limited in the area of diplomacy is a growing domain of concern between states who prefer to explore knowledge and competencies that endures farther of the ambit of the state engine bound for accomplishing development cooperation. Henceforward, there should be a creative synergy between the state and CSOs that can help in the performance of Indian diplomacy to think outside the box and improve the soft power of the country.

3.7 The post-COVID Indian Civil Society

Post-COVID state responses to the pandemic have disordered civil society globally. Social distancing measures and lockdown are restricting individuals to remain at home and limiting their strength to gather, coordinate, and advocate. Several CSOs have been compelled to put prospective projects on hold; others are clambering to shift their work online[135]. In many countries, prohibitive laws already had been clutching CSOs before the pandemic hit. Hence, the pandemic has given a suitable cover for states to moreover shift the balance of power in their favor[136]. During times of humanitarian emergency and emergency, CSOs with community awareness and local channels are well positioned to reach out to helpless communities. However even though some states are moving on to civil society's strength to augment their responses, several local organizations already communicate that public officials are bent on maintaining centralized power and have overlooked to discuss with them[137].

CSOs are going past assistance provision to begin attempting to hold states to account for inefficient or undemocratic crisis responses. CSOs at both the global and state levels are observing and articulating out against proceedings of exploitation of power[138]. In modern times, CSOs in many countries have encountered questions and suspicions about their legitimacy. Despite this, still, civic organizations advance in delivering quintessential assistance to affected societies and fill gaps in state responses where they may be able to expand their constituencies and social channels and eventually increase their legitimacy in the common core[139]. In the post-pandemic situation, civil society activism is likely to remain structured around reasonably professionalized and hierarchical state and global institutions[140]. Likewise, there is a need to bolster transnational support by the private and public actors who are committed to supporting CSOs to adapt to the new global setting through more magnanimous pandemic support packages, and strengthening policy stands on the importance of civil society regularly[141]. At the more widespread diplomatic level, the pandemic is a deciding moment to drive back against the anti-civil society narrative, which has grown so much terrain globally in the last decade[142].

Post- Covid Civil society's response to the pandemic in the country has contributed to significant assistance to the downtrodden and marginalized that had to be bolstered rather than subdued by the state. CSOs have come united to provide meals to the underprivileged and poor. Although the civil society response has demonstrated efficiency and effectiveness, hurdles and perplexities increase as space for civil society has been shrinking lately[143]. Due to the implementation of the FCRA Act, the state's response has been crotchety. This has led to unpropitious consequences on numerous CSOs where the state has taken stringent measures against civil society players, student leaders and suppressing civil rights activists. Post-lockdown, the country's difficulties have further complicated with many social ills such as economic disparity, hunger and poverty to name a few. Additionally there was unequal access to the public distribution system (PDS), lack of essentials, delayed arrival of supplies, bias and poor quality faced by families from marginalized populations. In this context, a survey states that NGOs in several Indian states have outperformed the state governments concerning free meals[144].

The "third sector" of the society or the civil society can perform a significant function in reducing the casualties from the pandemic[145]. Every nation has extensive, untapped assets in civil society that go beyond leaders and public employees. NITI Aayog reached out to nearly 92,000 NGOs and CSOs to promote cross-sectorial collaboration[146]. It is essential to note that if countries including India have to become resilient to pandemics, a more structured strategy is needed to use the untapped assets in civil society. States should likewise identify NGOs serving at the national and local level, which have the means to reach people to share important information, and also carry out welfare activities. In this context, mass education campaigns should be developed with the help of academicians, able scientists, and experts in the area of media and behavioral experts to increase awareness[147].

There has also been an increase in politically motivated proceedings brought by Indian officials under terrorism laws and relentless sedition against critics of the state. Unfortunately, many of the CSOs have been recognized for continuous and excellent pandemic work. Nevertheless, they are viewed skeptically by the state. Where several civil society activists have already been imprisoned following the lockdown time and remain to be held. Likewise, hurdles persevere due to thin linkages between societies, social institutions, low-income people and state governments. Various CSOs have also considered sealing down services due to the inadequacy of grants[148]. CSOs that were relying on CSR has also been facing larger obstacles because corporate funding has been redirected for pressing relief work and Prime Minister's Citizen Assistance and Relief in Emergency Situations (PM CARES) fund. If the government doesn't make efforts to amend the FCRA Act, this could have a tremendous adversarial bearing on already grappling CSOs and NGOs.

In the post-COVID scenario, a blend of 'soft power strategy and commitment through self-reliance approach, ease of doing business, education, culture, language, youth channels and deployment of economic establishments and methods to draw and sustain foreign investors will further assure India's just position and place globally. It is important to note that CSOs is a vital link between the state and the individual where the individuals come collectively in this domain. It represents the issues of the poor, the marginalized, the disadvantaged and the helpless. These linkages hold with them the ability to confront any rude authority of the state[149].

3.8 Conclusion

Civil society moreover has a prominent part in preventing majoritarian tendencies and preserving the substance of heterogeneity in India. The purpose of civil society in a tranquil world is fairly significant and harmony in the world will add to the success of India. However, some of the constraints of civil society are the intervention and involvement of the state parties, lack of adequate and equipped experts, bearing of different socioeconomic conditions in the nation such as casteism, poverty, non-cooperation by state leaders and bureaucrats, communalism etc. The commitments of democracy can solely be accomplished through cooperative action in civil society. A democratic state necessitates a democratic civil society and a democratic civil society likewise requires a democratic state. This co-operation reciprocally bolsters each other. Electoral amelioration, voter knowledge, and regular highlighting of the display of elected people should be crucial priority matters in civil society's plan. A robust and watchful civil society can also be a check on corruption and create the foundation for countervailing effect.

In a vast developing nation like India, there are many gaps neglected by the state in the growth method, which the civil societies require to permeate in contemporary India. Civil society can shape strategy and design formulation with the help of the association of committees and submission of memoranda. CSOs serve as an advocate of more vulnerable segments' viewpoint, an agent on part of aggrieved people, a watchdog against infringement of human rights and directing paucities, an administrator of citizens on their rights, entitlements and duties and the state about the throb of the people, mobiliser of public belief for or against a policy or plan and assistance provider to domains and citizens not reached by official purposes or as state's agent. India should indeed have an ideal civil society that must be the most robust critic of the state when necessary and at the same time be a gauge of the public. It should represent all the varied strata of a country's public. When the political parties are unresponsive, people can reach out to foci of influence and opportunity solely through an energetic civil society. A healthy civil society is therefore crucial for a healthy democracy.

India as a welfare nation is required to guarantee social justice simultaneously with economic growth. Laws should be implemented to accommodate civil society and people to seek relief. Personal liberties and rights have been safeguarded where many independent organizations are formed in the state. The peaceful co-existence of both the state and the civil society protects the interest of both the state and the citizens. The democratic character of the Indian civil society is shown in the establishment of a democratic state onward with the implementation of a democratic constitution. However, there is an unusual emergence of friction between the state and civil society as the requirements and expectations of the community are not met. Seldom, the state neglects the importance of the majority and meddles in the field of civil society. The phenomenon of a shrinking space for CSOs is today apparent in several countries due to the inward-looking nationalists. The new Financial Bill 2020 demands Indian NGOs to renew registrations every five years. Funds are frozen, news bulletins are selectively published to portray NGOs in a feeble light, and their movements are put on a surveillance list. Various schemes have been implemented for the elimination of poverty, reducing unemployment, malnutrition and too much bureaucratization has further led to red-tapism and corruption.

India that commemorated 70 years of democratic governance in 2017, is frequently portrayed as the world's biggest democracy and aspiring to be a $5trillion economy by 2025, and as such continues to be a reservoir of inspiration for communities' struggles for independence and human rights globally. The country parades an effective and vibrant civil society in various areas where CSOs are serving to hold the state to account for its decisions and developments and to push for policies that promote human rights and challenge segregation. The true nationalists of the country certainly picture India as a growing world leader in all likely domains. Therefore, in my opinion, India as an aspiring superpower and being the largest democracy globally should have good ties with the civil society to improve its over all image at the global platform. In this context, enhancing India's diplomacy and its soft power depends on the backbone of its state, economic progress and development. Though the present Indian government has done well in enhancing its ties with other nations and strengthening its diplomacy, unfortunately the country which calls itself as an ancient civilization and considers the world as a whole family at present hasn't been paying its attention to the domestic happenings in the country such as farmers issues, revoking of article 370 Jammu and Kashmir issue (J&K), citizenships rights etc. that has received criticism at the larger stage. India's evolving political environment in the last few years exhibits a pressing hurdle. To overcome this the GOI should remain in touch with public opinion and represent the will of the people at the grassroots level. India's route to world leadership is based on adhering to the political and economic needs of other nations too. In this context, in New Delhi, foreign policy circles, both MEA and the think tanks should skill themselves to consider this fact. India's existing soft power is the commitment to democracy, and professional activists are indispensable to it[150].

Lastly, for India to become the "soft power super-power" in the coming years, it should realize that unless there is no proper balance, co-operation and advancement at the domestic and civil society level with regard to important indicators of soft power such as education, health, gender equality, environment, media, governance etc. the country can not enhance its image at the international platform despite aiming to be one of the top economies in the world. An all-inclusive society is the right path for an aspiring super power like India. Hence, the role of CSOs as the backbone of the democracy in the coming years is very crucial for the country's all-inclusive society where the former's presence cannot be ignored. A democratic state requires a democratic civil society and a democratic civil society likewise requires a democratic state. Therefore, they jointly bolster each other.

Notes

1. Mahalingam (2018) *Governance in India*. New Delhi: Pearson India publication
2. *Ibid.*
3. *Ibid.*
4. *Ibid.*
5. *Ibid.*
6. Ibrahim, S (1998), Nurturing Civil Society at the World Bank, *Social development papers,* The World Bank, paper 24.
7. *Ibid.*
8. *Ibid.*
9. Mahalingam. (2018) *Governance in India*. New Delhi: Pearson India publication
10. *Ibid.*
11. *Ibid.*
12. Chandler (2004) *Constructing Global Civil Society: Morality and Power in International Relations*. London: Palgrave.
13. *Ibid.*
14. Donaldson. (2018) *A diplomatic deficit? The rise of non-state actors*. Available at: https://www.britishcouncil.org/research-policy-insight/insight-articles/diplomatic-deficit-actors (Accessed: 13 May 2020)
15. *Ibid.*
16. *Ibid.*
17. *Ibid.*
18. *Ibid.*
19. *Ibid.*
20. *Ibid.*
21. Marchetti, R (2016) *Global civil society*. Available at: https://www.e-ir.info/2016/12/28/global-Civil-society/ (Accessed: 23 December 2020)
22. *Ibid.*
23. *Ibid.*
24. Marchetti, R (2016) *Global civil society*. Available at: https://www.e-ir.info/2016/12/28/global-Civil-society/ (Accessed: 23 December 2020)
25. *Ibid.*
26. *Ibid.*

27. *Ibid.*
28. *Ibid.*
29. *Ibid.*
30. *Ibid.*
31. Nitisha. (2016) *Civil society in India and its role*. Available at: http://www.yourarticlelibrary.com/society/civil-society-in-india-and-its-role/47111/ (Accessed: 3 March 2020)
32. Arora. (2013) Good Governance: A Study of the Concept in Indian Context: Origin of the Concept of Good Governance, *Good Governance*, 37(1): 1-16
33. *Ibid.*
34. *Ibid.*
35. *Ibid.*
36. *Ibid.*
37. *Ibid.*
38. Hall, Pytlak. (2014) The Role of Civil Society in the International Negotiations on the Arms Trade Treaty, *Global Policy journal*, Vol. 5, Issue. 4, Pages 453-468, DOI: 10.1111/1758-5899.12173.
39. *Ibid.*
40. *Ibid.*
41. Das, S.K. (2007) Conflict and peace in India's North-east: The role of civil society, East-West Center Washington, *The Policy Studies*: 42.
42. Ansari,H. (2016) *Civil Society*. New Delhi: Rupa publication.
43. *Ibid.*
44. *Ibid.*
45. *Ibid.*
46. *Ibid.*
47. *Ibid.*
48. Mehta, A. (2007) Working with NGOs. New Delhi: civil society voices.
49. Sharma, C.P. (2013) Civil society in India: Making good governance a reality, *Centre for civil society,* CCS Working Paper No.303
50. *Ibid.*
51. Ansari, H. (2016) *Citizen and Society*. New Delhi: Rupa publication.
52. *Ibid.*
53. *Ibid.*
54. Singh, R. (2014) *Civil Society and Policymaking in India: In Search of Democratic Spaces*. Available at: https://www.oxfamindia.org/sites/default/files/WP7-Civil-Scty-n-plcy-mkg-in-India.pdf (Accessed: 5 December 2019)
55. Mathur, S. (2016) *The Need for Civil Society in Good Governance.* Available at: https://rashtram.org/the-need-for-civil-society-in-good-governance/ (Accessed: 15 December 2019)
56. *Ibid.*

57. Gupta, Sen. (2018), Ethnicity and Development: A Civil Society Perspective from North East India, *Journal of Social and Political Sciences*, Vol.1, No.2, 297-305.
58. *Ibid.*
59. *Ibid.*
60. Hamid, A (2016) *Citizen and Society*. New Delhi: Rupa Publication.
61. Arora, R. (2020) *Rule-bound governance matters. Rule-bound governance matters*. Available at: https://www.dandc.eu/en/article/civil-society-space-shrinking-india-oda-agencies-should-consider-their-stance (Accessed: 6 August 2020)
62. *Ibid.*
63. *Ibid.*
64. TNN. (2014) *Foreign-funded NGOs stalling development*. Available at: https://timesofindia.indiatimes.com/india/foreign-funded-ngos-stalling-development-ib-report/articleshow/36411169.cms (Accessed: 19 November 2019)
65. Hamid. A (2016) *Citizen and Society.* New Delhi: Rupa Publication.
66. Bobb, D. (2011) *In search of civil society*. Available at: https://indianexpress.com/article/opinion/columns/in-search-of-civil-society/ (Accessed: 29 December 2020)
67. Jaitley, A (2011) *The Indian democracy has the strength to emerge stronger*. Available at: https://www.tribuneindia.com/2011/20110829/nation.htm#2 (Accessed: 2 December 2019)
68. Hamid, A (2016) *Citizen and Society*. New Delhi: Rupa Publication.
69. *Ibid.*
70. *Ibid.*
71. Berglund, H (2009) Civil Society in India: democratic space or the extension Of elite domination, *NUJS International Journal of Legal Studies and Research*, Working papers 2009:1.
72. *Ibid.*
73. *Ibid.*
74. *Ibid.*
75. Singh, V. (2012) An Analysis of Concept and Role of Civil Society in Contemporary India, *Global Journals Inc.*, Volume 12 Issue 7.
76. Sharma, S. (2007) India and the Agreement on Agriculture: Civil Society and Citizens' Engagement, *Institute of Development Studies*, IDS Working Paper 278.
77. *Poorest Areas Civil Society (PACS) programme: India* (2013), Available at: https://www.gov.uk/guidance/poorest-areas-civil-society-pacs-programme-india (Accessed: 9 December 2019)
78. Sinha, A. (2016) *International Solar Alliance could be climate change game-changer*. Available at: https://indianexpress.com/article/explained/international-solar-alliance-isa-could-be-the-climate-change-game-changer-renewable-energy-4378033/ (Accessed: 14 January 2020)

79. Shivangi. (2021) *17 Best NGOs For Women Empowerment In India*. Available at: https://www.iforher.com/motivation/society-women/14-ngo-working-for-women-empowerment-India/ (Accessed: 2 February 2022)

80. Tripathi, Gaur. (2021) Role of civil societies and NGOs in achieving women empowerment in India, *Ipleaders blog*, 16 January, Available at: https://blog.ipleaders.in/role-civil-societies-ngos-achieving-women-empowerment-India/ (Accessed 8 January 2022)

81. *Ibid.*

82. *Ibid.*

83. *Ibid.*

84. Syal, R (2011) Civil Society Organizations and Elementary Education Delivery in Madhya Pradesh, *Institute for Social and Economic Change*. Working Papers 268.

85. *Universal Declaration of Human Rights* (2005), Available at https://www.un.org/en/udhrbook/pdf/udhr_booklet_en_web.pdf (Accessed: 9 September 2020)

86. Berglund. (2009) Civil Society in India: democratic space or the extension of elite domination? *Working Papers 2009:1,* Stockholm University.

87. Sorensen, B (2020) *The role of civil society in ensuring education for all*. Available at: https://educationoutloud.org/role-civil-society-ensuring-education-all (Accessed: 4 July 2021)

88. *Ibid.*

89. *Ibid.*

90. *Ibid.*

91. Ghosh, M.D (2020) *Youth can be a clear advantage for India*. Available at: https://www.thehindu.com/opinion/lead/youth-can-be-a-clear-advantage-for-India/article30897179.ece (Accessed: 15 January 2021)

92. *Ibid.*

93. Davis, I. (2010) The Role of Civil Society and the Media', in Building Integrity and Reducing Corruption in Defence: A Compendium of Best Practices, *Geneva Centre for the Democratic Control of Armed Forces (DCAF)*, pp. 261-280.

94. *Ibid.*

95. Ansari, H (2016) *Citizen and society*, Rupa publication.

96. Sarkar P (2017) Role of Media in Strengthening Democracy in India, *J Adv Res* Jour Mass Comm, 4(3&4): 111-115.

97. Ibid.

98. The role of civil society and media (No date). Available at: https://egyankosh.ac.in/bitstream/123456789/63234/1/Unit-11.pdf (Accessed: March 6 2020)

99. *Ibid.*

100. *Ibid.*

101. *Ibid.*

102. *Ibid.*

103. Ansari, H(2016) *Citizen and society.* New Delhi: Rupa publication.

104. Pavlinai. (No date) *Civil Society in Internet Governance*. Available at: https://www.diplomacy.edu/project/civil-society-in-internet-governance/ (Accessed: 2 January 2021)

105. *Ibid.*

106. *Ibid.*

107. *Ibid.*

108. Ahmed, S. (2010) The Role of the Media During Communal Riots in India: A Study of the 1984 Sikh Riots and the 2002 Gujarat Riots, *Media Asia*, 37(2), 103-112.

109. Hon Dr Victor Dan-Jumbo, *Pillars of Democracy* (first published 2014, Hillsberg) 15

110. *Ibid.*

111. *Ibid.*

112. Ranjeet. (2018) Media as the Fourth Pillar of Democracy, *ipleaders blog*, 29 November, Available at: https://blog.ipleaders.in/media-as-a-fourth-pillar-of-democracy/ (Accessed 18 June 2020)

113. *Ibid.*

114. Panichi, P (2013) Civil Society and Non Official Diplomacy in Interregional Relations: The European Union and Asia, *European Institute for Asian Studies*, Briefing Paper 2013/1.

115. *Ibid.*

116. *Ibid.*

117. *Ibid.*

118 Srivastava, S (2016) Inside and outside India: Non-State actors and public diplomacy, *CPD blog,* 14 October. Available at: https://uscpublicdiplomacy.org/blog/inside-and-outside-india-non-state-actors-and-public-diplomacy (Accessed: 27 December 2020)

119. *Ibid.*

120. Gupta, S (2016) *The Role of Civil Society in Shaping India's Development Partnerships.* Available at: https://www.e-ir.info/2016/01/07/the-role-of-civil-society-in-shaping-indias-development-Partnerships/ (Accessed: 23 July 2020)

121. *Ibid.*

122. Balakrishnan. (2019) *Changing dynamics of Indian Foreign Policy: the Science and Technology Dimension.* Available at: https://www.mea.gov.in/distinguished-lectures-Detail.htm? 846 (Accessed: 9 January 2020)

123. *Ibid.*

124. Secches, Aires. (2016) Civil society and regional powers in a changing world: The cases of Brazil and India, *Brazilian Journal of Strategy & International Relations*, 5(10). DOI: 10.22456/2238-6912.65081

125. *Ibid.*

126. *Ibid.*

127. *Ibid.*

128. *Ibid.*

129. Hall, Pytlak. (2014) The Role of Civil Society in the International Negotiations on the Arms Trade Treaty, *Global Policy journal*, Vol. 5, Issue. 4, Pages 453-468, DOI: 10.1111/1758-5899.12173.

130. Zeeshan, M (2021) *India's diplomatic corps is understaffed, busy with bureaucratic work. That's a problem.* Available at: https://theprint.in/pageturner/excerpt/indias-diplomatic-corps-is-understaffed-busy-with-bureaucratic-work-thats-a-problem/589685/ (Accessed: 5 April 2022)

131. *Ibid.*

132. Tirkey, A (2020) *The NEST: A pragmatic addition to India's external affairs ministry*. Available at: https://www.orfonline.org/expert-speak/the-nest-a-pragmatic-addition-to-indias-external-affairs-ministry-63864/ (Accessed: 9 April 2021)

133. Gupta, S. (2016) *The Role of Civil Society in Shaping India's Development Partnerships.* Available at: https://www.e-ir.info/2016/01/07/the-role-of-civil-society-in-shaping-indias-development-partnerships/ (Accessed: 12 April 2020)

134. *Ibid.*

135. Youngs, et.al (2020) *Civil Society and the Coronavirus: Dynamism Despite Disruption*. Available at: https://carnegieendowment.org/2020/04/21/civil-society-and-coronavirus-dynamism-despite-disruption-pub-81592 (Accessed: 12 April 2021)

136. *Ibid.*

137. *Ibid.*

138. *Ibid.*

139. *Ibid.*

140. *Ibid.*

141. *Ibid.*

142. *Ibid.*

143. Rustagi, Wu. (2020) *Indian civil society sidelined in a pandemic*. Available at: https://www.eastasiaforum.org/2020/10/30/indian-civil-society-sidelined-in-a-pandemic/East Asia (Accessed: 3 April 2021)

144. *Ibid.*

145. Singh. (2020) *Civil Society: The third pillar of strength in fight against coronavirus*. Available at: https://government.economictimes.indiatimes.com/news/governance/civil-society-the-third-pillar-of-strength-in-fight-against-coronavirus/75642349 (Accessed: 4 April 2021)

146. *Ibid.*

147. *Ibid.*

148. *Ibid.*

149. *Ibid.*

150. Yadav, P (2021) *India's real soft power is commitment to democracy, and 'andolanjeevis' are integral to it.* Available at: https://theprint.in/campus-voice/indias-real-soft-power-is-commitment-to-democracy-and-andolanjeevis-are-integral-to-it/610552/ (Accessed: 18 April 2022)

Chapter Four

Indian Elephant and Chinese Dragon - A Soft Power Comparison

4.1 China's Soft Power: An Introduction

China, officially known as the Peoples Republic of China (PRC), is a country in East Asia, being the world's most populated country. It is considered an influential global player with its second-largest economy. The Chinese Communist Party (CCP) is the founding and governing political party of contemporary China. In 2012, since president Xi Jinping came to power, he has amalgamated his power over the CCP party, with several experts naming him the most influential Chinese leader ever since Mao Zedong[1]. Every Chinese leader has catchphrases that act as a model of one's policies and an approach for the people[2]. Therefore, president Xi announced that his first catchphrase would be "Chinese dream where he brought it in line with the "American dream"[3]. This also saw the setting up of a contemporary socialist state with Chinese elements to which Xi noted the Chinese dream with the resurgence of Chinese civilization comprising of China and its people[4]. President Xi urged the delegates at the party's 19th congress to, "Tell the China story well and build China's soft power"[5]. Thus, presently, the Chinese State media has further rapidly grown their overseas operations, while the CCP has driven patriotic videos on western social media platforms[6].

This chapter focuses on China's soft power and advances further with its challenges. Later, the chapter makes a comparison between India and China's soft power and progresses further to mention about the soft power of both the countries in the post-COVID era.

4.2 The Soft Power of China

Napoleon Bonaparte once said of China, "Let her sleep, for when she wakes, she will shake the world[7]." Today, China's rise has been a matter of argument among scholars of international political economy (IPE) and IR for nearly two decades[8]. China has evolved from a country of predominantly impoverished peasants to a financial powerhouse, paramount to the global economy and second in size only to the U.S[9]. The last few decades have seen a fast transformation of China's position in international security and economic matters that had a significant impact which was not welcomed with global readiness[10]. According to U.S journalist Joshua Kurlantzick, "as China constructed an international approach, it has furthermore evolved more worldly instruments of leverage, which it deploys globally"[11]. China's rise since the early 1990s has been viewed in the U.S, from a structural standpoint by neo-realists who see it as a "power shift" competent to reshaping the global balance of power at the international and regional levels[12]. The growth of China's "overall power" has become an essential part impacting the setting of IR in the 21st century[13]. The instruments of "China's soft power" are culture and diplomacy that are deployed and supported by means of the country's rising economic strength[14]. The determinants of China's foreign policy include tradition, ideology, capabilities, diplomacy and intelligent operation[15]. The country's foreign policy has likewise been influenced by internal and external factors[16]. Internal factors include the population being influenced by the global community like media outlets such as radio, television, Internet etc. and external factors include China's influence in the UNSC, its business ties with International Monetary Fund (IMF) and World Bank[17]. The State Council Information Office of China (SCIO) is the prominent official organ of China's cultural diplomacy and the Bureau for External Cultural Relations Ministry of China is another state organ that is in charge of the country's cultural diplomacy[18]. For CCP, after politics and economics, culture has been regarded as the third pillar of Chinese diplomacy with the 11th five-year strategy insisting on a more distinguished presence of China in international cultural markets[19].

Power has been an aspect of IR studies since the earlier writings by Machiavelli and Thucydides and is perhaps one of the most significant and least comprehended concepts in IR[20]. China as a "status quo power" also raises the question for many countries[21]. The country has been advancing the democratization of IR in the new global order since the late 1990s[22] and has been associated with discrete policy objectives such as facilitating Chinese firms, growing political players and alleviating apprehensions about China's economic advancement[23]. Nevertheless, China's rising soft power could prove benign or even advantageous in some respects[24].

China's discontentment with the existing architecture has been directed toward creating completely new institutions and initiatives such as the BRI, and AIIB placing China in the mainstream decision-making position to the exclusion of the west[25]. While there is no sign China is serious about the hegemonic obstacles and will further work towards system transformation but not overpower[26].

Political authorities and IR scholars have been verbal about China's military expansion and what it could demand for the future[27]. A rising power's impact on the status-quo rule has been a problem for geopolitics, geo-economics, global legal studies and other domains for a long time[28]. Presently, China has startled the world with a considerable expansion in military, cultural, economic, and geopolitical factors[29]. Constructing pro-China global organizations such as the AIIB and extending its power in pro-western organizations shows the expansion of Chinese sway in the international economic system[30].

China's remarkable growth after Deng Xiaoping's economic reforms in 1978 laid the bases for some definite accomplishments that have guided to 'rise of China' spectacle as shown by institutions such as the U.N, which notes a profound transformation in international dynamics and evolving geopolitics[31]. If one sees the all-around development of the IR in China, it can be argued that the Maoist years primarily concentrated on constructing a new state[32]. The Chinese context of power was integrated with the ideological justifications of Mao's thinking within a realist foreign policy[33]. Besides using cultural elements, China today uses trade, investment and aid to expand its power and influence[34].

From the definitions of soft power provided by Nye, Wang and Lu, there are four general categories that a nation must achieve to influence soft power effectively: ideology, institutions, culture and foreign policy[35]. In this context, CCP has not restricted itself to regional institutions and as a member of the UNSC China has sent many peacekeeping soldiers[36]. Foreign policy is a complicated, yet vital tenet of soft power[37]. In the case of CCP, one can notice that soft power, for the most part heads foreign policy where the leadership tries to expand its soft power via its foreign policies[38]. One of the most important aspects of soft power is making the country's culture and ideology attractive to other countries where the objective is to make one's culture a global norm as per Nye[39]. Despite China's limited role in influencing developing countries, its soft power enabled it to achieve a foothold in the global community as a leader[40]. As a part of China's 'going out and 'going global' strategy, China has also uplifted the mainstream media to improve the scope and forge possible optimistic leverage on global thought[41]. China's foreign currency reserves likewise have helped the country to deliver substantial levels of development aid and grant besides a fast-growing middle class[42]. China in the foreseeable future is expected to play a much greater role in a broader range of organizational and institutional matters[43]. China's capability to impact and potentially move the policies and practices of multilateral institutions is increasing, although institutional hindrances to dominant Chinese influence are nevertheless challenging[44].

Kurlantzick further opines that soft power is strong by indicating that it describes anything beyond the military and security domain, consisting not merely public diplomacy and popular culture but also additionally coercive economic and diplomatic levers like investment and aid and participation in multilateral institutions[45]. The Nation-states are increasingly certain about the significance of integrating political and economic capacities with other 'soft' resources for extending their areas of influence and attaining global plausibility[46]. While the idea has its bases in U.S president Roosevelt's view of 'speak softly and carry a stick', China has been one of the most dynamic employers of 'smart power' in the contemporary period[47].

Furthermore, China's participation in different multilateral and regional platforms such as the SCO, ASEAN and BRICS shows its readiness to change and function with myriad associations and partners[48]. Nye's focus on culture as the essence of soft power sees the increasing resonance in China's conduct of external engagement[49]. China's measure to connect with its diaspora has been instrumental given its contributions to domestic economic growth, scientific innovations and higher education[50]. China believes further in the role of the diaspora in actively spreading Chinese civilization and vigorously promoting the ties between China and the global population[51]. The contemporary Chinese foreign policy in its international and regional dimensions is distinctive in depicting China as a peace-loving, pro-people, harmonious, tolerant, confident and accountable power[52]. The post-Tiananmen Chinese scholarly literature indicates a growing interest in the country's soft power[53].

Due to the fast development and growth of its economy, China is poised to challenge, and potentially surpass, the U.S as the predominant power[54]. The policy elites and scholars of China appear to also have positioned a high premium on enhancing and expanding the country's media transmission ability and the persuasiveness of its mass communications[55]. This is due to the continued mistrust of China toward the western media, which is seen as innately aggressive and prejudiced[56].

4.3 Challenges of China's Soft Power

China is an age-old civilization with nearly 3,500 years of documented history[57]. With the country's growing economic power, assertive nationalism, and regional interests, a harsh realist strategy will heighten Chinese security problems and probably lead to military conflict[58]. The "China Threat" in the west has been associated by IR neo-realists with security predicament and hegemonic transition[59]. Realist scholars assert that a growing economy will necessarily push China to challenge the "status quo"[60]. China's economic advancement has forced questions concerning China's urge to challenge the present status quo and expand territorially, military and in effect[61].

IR scholars and policymakers are grappling with the implications of China's rise that would make China adopt an increasingly bold and competitive approach[62]. Chinese foreign policy has consistently been shaped by its ultimate leader's ideas[63]. According to Mersheimer, China cannot rise peacefully and the fundamental presumption of his "offensive realism" is a bold one where he describes great powers as revisionist predators in pursuit of survival[64]. The foremost aim of any powerful state is to achieve regional hegemony and China's efforts to construct artificial islands in the South China Sea (SCS) are viewed as expansionist and aggressive by its neighbors[65]. The CCP seeks to establish regional hegemony and use the SCS to project power in-depth into the Pacific[66]. Nevertheless, constructivist variables like country history and the rising power identity serve a secondary role in revamping the strategy[67].

Also, socializing has been a sluggish and tortuous procedure, particularly for an ancient civilization like China[68]. For most western viewers and decision-makers, who look for immediate outcomes, associating with China can be a tedious movement because China at times seems to be accountable and at times not[69].

Presently, the world is in a crucial era of transformation, therefore international issues and contemporary challenges demand the world to seek answers distinct from those of the earlier era[70]. 'Harmonious world', for instance, is a notion profoundly embedded in the conventional culture of China for several thousand years though Chinese political leaders have lately brought it out as an ideal global order[71]. Therefore, Chinese IR scholars assert that Chinese culture can contribute theoretically to the establishment of such a global order[72].

However, China's emphasis on constructing a harmonious world has decreased and a greater focus on protecting its "core interests" (territorial integrity) such as Tibet, Taiwan and Xinjiang issues has become an important part of China's accounts, which involve hard power and realism[73]. China's rise has started to present a significant challenge to the liberal democracy based on individual rights, rule of law and multi-party elections[74]. This was exemplified in the 2000s when Beijing blocked off China from the Internet and instituted its own Internet known as "Great Firewall of China[75]". China is still struggling with transforming its soft power resources into substantial changes in the global view[76]. Some scholars have also claimed that enhancing China's soft power demands to be supplemented with more Chinese elements[77]. Today, China's IR is usually uplifted by a desire to recapture the lost glory of the "Middle Kingdom" and via soft power strategies, Beijing has discovered a route to achieving this by uncovering pathways to enhance its global footprint[78]. The usage of soft power in China's past has barely been a contemporary story[79]. Admiral Zheng He during the Ming Dynasty wielded soft power by travelling across the Indian Ocean and the South China Sea by paying a visit to several countries to show the riches and influence of the Ming Dynasty considered a charm offensive in its own way[80].

Presently, China in multiple contexts may not be pursuing a whole soft power approach though may in some instances be observing a "Sharp Power" approach as well[81]. If China is clearly being more confrontational in its territorial aims, this may give way to the "sharp power" theory where China is utilizing soft power to expand its territorial dominance using segments of force and flexing military power to accomplish that end[82]. Sharp power, a term coined by Cardenal in 2017, is wielded by authoritarian governments to manipulate media, culture and education[83]. In recent years, the foreign policy of China may have shifted from "soft power" to "sharp power"[84]. Nye has further asserted "Chinese soft power" as a failure, when he defined getting others to want what you want[85]. In this context, he stated that China wants soft power but judging by its propaganda, doesn't know how to get it[86]. Despite the "China dream", the Hong Kong protests have indicated that China still knows hard power much better than soft where, China risks deteriorating what little soft power it has[87]. Nye has likewise downplayed the country's capability to improve its soft power[88]. He claimed that due to a dearth of intellectual freedom, unmellow cultural endeavor and political degeneration, China's soft power despite being culturally appealing could not be projected overseas as compared to the U.S or Europe[89]. Also, China has been channelizing principles to malign democracies and encourage an authoritarian governance model globally by showing its economic development[90].

Furthermore, Realism thinker, Morgenthau had cited three power instruments available to statesmen to promote their national interests, which are threats, bribes and logic[91]. Therefore, China through its "Chequebook diplomacy" has long been accused of gaining favor with countries globally[92]. Later, Neo-realists put forth the intricacy of the system to its polarizing factor[93]. To comprehend IR as per neo-realists, one must examine the diffusion of power across the world nexus and the applicability of its players[94]. As per neo-realism, the three types of polarity are unipolarity, bipolarity and multipolarity[95]. In this context, China is said to have a part in all three[96]. Neo-realism is considered an ideal theory that seeks to explain what China is attempting to achieve through "Debt-trap diplomacy"[97]. Debt traps considered keystones of neo-realism are a way of exerting authority and dominance over the community struggling with an economic deficit[98]. China's BRI has led to debt for infrastructure deals, which nevertheless, further China's geostrategic claims by expanding its international presence and leverage[99]. For instance, Pakistan and Sri Lanka being the major beneficiary of financial aid from China have plunged into political and economic disarray[100]. The Pacific nations have likewise been vulnerable due to the "debt-trap diplomacy"[101]. The lack of transparency about the BRI limits objective authentic economic estimation of the problem and raises doubts regarding the commercial terms of China's lending[102]. As per the United Nations Conference on Trade and Development (UNCTAD) report of 2021, Sri Lanka has suffered a dearth of long-term finance in manufacturing and infrastructure due to which BRI has been seen as "debt-trap diplomacy" by the U.S for all poorer and developing countries[103].

With the emergence of China as a chief financier in African infrastructure, the former is utilizing debt to achieve geopolitical influence by entrapping impoverished nations in unsustainable loans[104]. Due to this, Africa's increasing public debt has resulted in a continued international debate about debt sustainability in Africa[105]. China's sudden interest in Africa has increased anxiety in some quarters labeling the country's acts in Africa as "neo-colonialist"[106]. Africa is also seeing a slowdown in economic growth due to China's loans where many African nations are re-negotiating loan terms with China where, lately, the debts have led to a repayment crisis[107]. Think tanks and scholars correspondingly view BRI as a geopolitical and diplomatic offensive sought at rewriting the contemporary geopolitical setting[108]. Also, espionage, interference and even torture allegations are infuriating China's ties with some of the top democracies globally even as China aims to persuade countries that its 5G technology can be trusted[109]. Due to such issues, in the recent years, as per the Pew Research, the views of China have grown more negative in several advanced economies with an unfavorable opinion of China[110].

Since Xi came to power in 2012, China has been under great pressure due to the crackdown on several CSOs besides many activists being arrested, sentenced to prison or detained[111]. The authoritative system of CCP has a monopoly on the state power and dominates considerable parts of society like media, judicial system, civil society, education, government and bureaucracy[112]. This is in contrast to liberal democracies in which activists engage through lobbying elected politicians and advocacy through public hearings, which is not possible in China[113]. Therefore, an active strategy for the politics of civil society engagement is crucial to grasp how the changes in political space will impact the forms and spaces of engagement in the coming years[114]. Nonetheless, CCP's further crackdown on freedom of expression, civil society and independent thought currently expands further its territories[115]. In the U.N, China has likewise misused its seat on the UNESCO Committee on NGO Committee to stop applications from CSOs pursuing U.N consultative status[116]. The Chinese diplomats have further blocked applications from NGOs working on human rights issues and have asked applicants to explicitly acknowledge Tibet and Taiwan as an essential part of China[117]. CCP has thus cracked down on CSOs and aimed to sever associations between global and domestic NGOs[118]. China, in 2016, also passed new laws on foreign NGOs amid criticism where the law was incidentally aimed at smothering civil society further[119].

The seismic transformation in global geopolitics caused by China's emergence as an international power has prompted a significant drive in studying, understanding and anticipating what it implies for other states and the international order[120]. The "peaceful rise" versus the "China threat" demonstrates an ongoing policy predicament for several states[121]. The CCP has been showcasing "sharp power" by using Confucius Institutes (CIs) to gain foothold in universities overseas. Some observers have also associated CI's to "Trojan horses"[122]. CI's are a non-profit organization aimed at promoting Chinese culture and language has been reprimanded for pressuring host universities to censor speeches known to be politically sensitive to China. For instance, a U.S university cancelled its plan to invite Dalai Lama, a Tibetan spiritual leader for a talk. Another university removed a reference to Taiwan from a University speaker's biography[123]. Presently, many countries have ordered the closure of CI's and Chinese supported cultural and language programmes in various institutions[124]. The CCP has also been criticized for human rights abuses under International law and crimes against Turkic Muslims and Uighurs' in the Xinjiang region[125].

Realism that is primarily concerned with matters of state security and authority is likewise said to be an IR perspective for comprehending cyber warfare[126]. Realism presents questions about cyber power, how it is connected to international stability and who retains it[127]. Cyber operations have become China's instrument of choice to achieve proprietary Intellectual Property Rights (IPR) and collect personal data globally[128]. Due to this, democracies have responded to China's sharp power and information warfare[129]. According to Nye, in a democratic system, much of the soft power is derived from civil society, which is an important asset[130]. However, if China wants to enhance its soft power it ought to soften some of its tight party control over civil society[131]. Also, dependence on covert channels of communication and manipulation of media often decreases soft power[132].

Furthermore, the Chinese films stay solely a China only endeavor since even its former Asian neighbors who are part of the Confucian ring refuse to screen these movies[133]. The instrument to cinematic soft power resides in awakening fascination instead of dictating it[134]. China should embrace a softer strategy to soft power rather than toughening its soft power approach[135]. Population ageing will additionally continue to pose grave challenges to China's socio-economic sustainability and lead to the disappearance of the demographic dividend[136].

Power is hard to define[137]. It is like the weather where everyone relies on it and talks about it, though few comprehend it[138]. China generally uses the term "Wai Xuan" known as external propaganda to promote the country's accomplishments and enhance its vision overseas[139]. Though China is particularly thriving in "Nei Xuan" known as interior propaganda, it is relatively weak in "Wai Xuan" known as exterior propaganda and the basis for this is the merging of exterior and interior propaganda by the CCP[140]. Many Chinese authors indicate that CCP has more additionally to accomplish, to create a great impact that China has in mind[141]. The CCP has a communist ideology that lacks legitimacy and cannot draw democratic countries to support its path[142]. Thus, China rather utilizes coercion to impact the behavior of others[143]. If China requires acceptance from the world, it needs to develop the principles of liberty, respect for human rights, the rule of law and the basic freedom to construct a national image that is more appealing to the international audience[144]. Correspondingly, the compromise with Dalai Lama could become an effective basis of soft power for China[145]. U.S Sinologist, Shambaugh asserts that though China spends approximately $10 billion a year notwithstanding its endeavors, China is yet to see a substantial return on its investment[146]. As CCP celebrated its

100th anniversary in 2021, it faces hurdles overseas and within the country such as COVID-19, economic inequality and many other difficulties.

6.4 The Soft Power of India and China

China and India were considered the most populous regions of the world a thousand years ago[147]. Both the countries have experienced a long process of economic reforms although the process has been more progressive in China[148]. Furthermore, the Rise of Confucianism in China greatly mixed with India's Buddhism to develop a distinctive cultural and philosophical synergy between the two civilizations[149]. Nonetheless, both countries were forced back strategically and economically[150]. Also, their civilizational amicability deteriorated with the advancement of European imperialism, specifically the British Empire in India[151]. However, India, compared to China has consistently made use of soft power diplomacy[152]. Since it's Independence, India has shown more preference for soft power, unlike China[153]. It was only post-2000s that China enhanced its soft power, which later became an integral part of Chinese foreign policy[154]. However, today, compared to China, which is undemocratic in nature, Indian culture enjoys great popularity globally though more needs to be done to enhance the soft power of India[155]. Nevertheless, soft power needs to be earned without unnatural interference from the state and cannot be bought[156]. In this context, China shows decreasing attempts to influence opinion overseas and easing constraints inside the country[157].

Nye acknowledges that soft power is a 'staple' of democratic politics, while China is an authoritative system[158]. Like many other scholars, Nye asserts that 'states should abstain from direct interference in soft power assets as the civil society ought to play a significant function[159]. Nye also states that soft power depends on the receiving end since attractiveness lies in the eyes of the beholder and what is appealing for some people is not necessarily appealing to others[160]. Therefore, a country should be aware of its attractive elements where some features may be useful and appreciated in some contexts and not in others[161]. Today, the Indian cultural exports in have led to the perception of the "non-threatening rise of India", creating a remarkable amenity about India and things Indian[162]. China's 'peaceful rise' is an illusion due to its 'aggressive rise' in contrast to India's great power ambitions that promote 'non-coercive' or 'soft power' progression[163]. As per Xinbo, a Chinese scholar, China is mostly a "traditional regional power rather than an "International power" and thus lacks real global thinking in international diplomatic activism and its foreign policy[164].

China and India in the 21st century symbolize outstanding cultural nations that are trying to become prominent political powers[165]. China has had a prosperous and strong History and Mao like Confucius was a creative transmitter of tradition, excavating the country's cultural elements for answers to modern plights[166]. China presently has undergone remarkable success and poverty decline[167]. The former Singapore PM Lee Kuan Yew stated that 'soft power is attained solely when other countries admire and want to emulate parts of that country's civilization'[168]. The immense changes in the international economy also helped advance not just an Asian financial boom but likewise directed an eastward motion and competition of international influence and power due to Asia's rise to the global system and the likely emergence of a new multi-polar order[169]. While both countries are emerging powers in the global system they still suffer from unequal development from within and they also have some of the highest levels of inequality in the world besides being filled with uncertainties[170]. CCP since 1996 called for the establishment of the New Security Concept (NSC) emphasized soft power diplomacy through discussion, dialogue and partnership[171]. NSC later has become an essential element of the foreign policy of China[172]. However, an opposing critical school in China has called for a more assertive and bold foreign policy matching China's standing as a global power[173]. Also, It is important for India to critically balance China's rising power[174]. Though successful in its engagement, there is likewise invariably a possible danger of an anti-Sino surge against Chinese national interests[175]. Nevertheless, China is correspondingly anticipated to hold a similar "hard and soft" blend in its foreign policy towards the rest of the nations in the region[176]. This is also presumably to be greatly defined by China's growing relations with India[177]. The future path of Chinese soft power in South Asia will likewise depend greatly on the shifts taking place in China's strategic foci for the region following shifts in its equations with India[178]. The increasing participation of China in IO's further delivers a commencement and influence of its expanding power and a step of its advanced international duties and commitments[179]. The complex identity of China as a developing superpower, a permanent member of the UNSC exerting a veto, a member of the premier P-5 (Permanent Five) nuclear association and a socialist country earlier exploited by imperialist nations has led to contradicting problems and distinctive conduct[180]. China's political culture and Marxist principles continue to shape its Individual motivations and perceptions and the answers to global institutions[181].

Furthermore, India is probably China's closest soft power 'competitor'. For China, culture has been inseparable from politics, underlining the specificity of the context and a central position by state actors in CD nearly inherently[182]. Such distinction is not observable in India where cultural transmission has traditionally comprised more non-state actors[183]. However, while India seems reluctant and baffled in boosting the appropriate blend of hard and soft power, China has been belligerent and careful in incorporating hard and soft power[184]. The Asian Literature demonstrates soft power in its earliest form. Lao Tse's famous quote: "Water is the softest thing, yet it can penetrate mountains and earth", denotes the principle clearly how softness overpowers hardness[185]. Even the famous ancient Indian realist thinker, Chanakya stated how to win neighboring powers by non-aggression and appeasement and through gift, which denotes the importance of soft power in ancient Indian politics[186].

Formulating diplomacy and engagement in Asia has become more strategically complicated. As growing powers and Asian countries, China and India acknowledge this more than anyone else. But, as India and China celebrated their 70th anniversary of bilateral ties in 2020, both countries have been caught in border disputes on the Line of Actual Control (LAC) such as the 1962 Sino-India war, the 2017 Doklam conflict and the recent Galwan issue[187]. India as a rising power should also continue to maintain the "status quo" unlike China's attempts to alter the status quo[188]. Nevertheless, India and China as rising powers must consider displaying the "2018 Wuhan Spirit"[189]. Dutta asserts, "India's ties with China are uncertain in the best of times, while over the previous few years the range of disparities between the two largest nations has gradually become complicated[190]. China has adopted "offensive realism" while India followed "defensive realism"[191]. China would unlikely trigger military action against other regional states. Instead, it would try to assure that it dominates through force and economic power[192]. China, moreover, plans to retrieve its historical standing at the top of a tributary system, though in a contemporary form[193]. Due to China's hegemonic acts, India has therefore sought "defensive realism" by joining partnerships, not alliances, with several western and regional countries to balance China's power[194]. Two civilizational states growing simultaneously and sharing a border crisis is unparalleled in the history of the world[195]. China and India both want international power standing and authority in their individual regions, while China's offensive realism rejects its capacity to recognize India as a rising power in its own right[196]. For China, resolving the border conflict with India is a problem led by caution[197]. China's geographical insecurities concerning Tibet will remain as long as the Sino-Indian boundary is not determined[198]. But, India unlike China desires peaceful coexistence and facilitates discussion and dialogue to settle all disputes.

The PD through media can recreate a formative part in boosting mutual understanding and both the countries are aware that harmony and cooperation are paramount[199]. Some media channels have been more determined on spreading the flames than concentrate on the links that tie the two age-old civilizations[200]. Presently, India and China's state branding measures include global messaging via strategic and broadcasting communications, promoting cultural exchanges, revving digital diplomacy and people to people contact[201]. But, India requires strengthening its federal system, encouraging more NGOs by guaranteeing its smooth functioning and also maintaining its long-cherished secular values[202]. Soft power becomes powerful solely when it is multiplied to project the notion of an unbiased, democratic, vibrant, progressive society that is a responsible stakeholder in global politics and a supporter of the international public good[203]. India requires investing adequately to ensure the effectiveness of soft power[204]. For instance, as the largest democracy, India does not have a global television channel like the British Broadcasting Corporation (BBC) or Al Jazeera that showcases the country globally[205]. India's national channel, such as "Doordarshan" needs be revived to go International[206]. However, presently, World Is One News (WION) is the first global English new network owned by India that has reached over 190 countries[207]. Also, China through its media network, China Central Television (CCTV) has also rebranded as a global "soft power" to increase the country's influence globally[208]. A senior CCP member amidst the negativity in Sino-India relations in 2016 underscored the necessity for the media in both countries to build on the "positive energies" in bilateral ties to improve collective confidence and bring the two Asian giants nearer[209]. Also, former Indian foreign affairs minister Swaraj emphasized the role media can play to enhance relations between China and India by further stating that media in each country has its national characteristic referring to a greatly autonomous Indian media as compared to the Chinese state-run media[210]. Swaraj underlined the contributions of ancient scholars such as India's Kumarajiva and Xuanzang of China in enhancing ties[211].

The roots of contemporary day Chinese public diplomacy can be traced to the 1950s[212]. Under Hu Jintao and his successor Xi, China has paid more awareness to public diplomacy as it pursues to rebrand its position on the global podium[213]. Through the "going out" strategy, there was an investment of billions of dollars annually in the international expansion of Chinese media[214]. However, by 2012, the country's domestic media and NGO exchanges were already under tighter party control and the centralized CCP establishment remained in terms of public diplomacy[215]. China has also been involved in para-diplomatic activities[216]. Recent literature on China's Para-diplomacy has pointed out that while overseas affairs powers of its provinces have increased, provincial governments remain sensitive in leading overseas engagements and will not infringe on foreign agendas[217]. The present GOI has also demonstrated a paradigm shift in India's foreign policy-making by admiring the vital function that States can play in the conduct of diplomacy[218]. India's earlier attempts at soft power projection include the formation of public diplomacy within the MEA in 2006 and the launch of the 'Incredible India' tourism campaign[219]. Also, the Know India Programmes (KIP) is a significant endeavor of the GOI to engage and make the students and young professionals of the Indian Diaspora feel a sense of connection with India's forms of culture, heritage and art[220]. India and China both also have a large diaspora population[221]. Thus, the contribution of Diasporas is likely to become more important in the 21st century to woo their immigrants[222]. Chinese and Indians are regarded as two of the primary "international tribes" who have accomplished economic victory in modern international political economy[223]. Language, considered the soul of civilization and the spirit of a country has also played a greatly important role in the India-China exchange[224]. Indian languages like Pali, Sanskrit, Hindi, Bengali etc. are some of the majors offered at Peking University, China[225]. However, educational and cultural offerings between both countries are still at the ground level and need more push including cultural exchanges at the NGOs on the border of both sides[226].

India and China has also made impact in "Animal diplomacy". India followed "Elephant Diplomacy" post-independence and sent several elephants to many countries[227]**.** Known to be a potent instrument of diplomacy in engaging with several countries, PM Nehru, in 1949, sent a baby elephant named after his daughter Indira[228]. Lately, as per the news reports, not many Indian leaders have taken an active interest in this practice and revived this tradition[229]. In China, pandas, known to be a symbol of peace for China are considered to be a key to foreign relations via soft power[230]. The panda is regarded to be a symbol of China parallel to how the dragon is considered the symbol of its nationalism[231]. Unlike the Confucius Institutes, pandas are well accepted by countries globally and pandas have also been used as themes for Chinese movies[232]. Recently, China celebrated the 50th anniversary of Panda diplomacy[233].

Nation-states have a variety of ways to deploy soft power to shape others' preferences and attitudes[234]. IR scholars have been rather slow in analyzing the linkages between soft power, tourism and foreign policy[235]. China has quickly become the most popular tourist destination for many nations measured by the number of trips[236]. Tourism has performed a vital role in increasing the soft power of a country, which thus makes a country admirable. China has no dearth of soft power instruments. The country is the second most UNESCO World Heritage site in the world besides excelling in Olympics. China's success in the usage of soft power can be noticed particularly in two areas such as tourism and international student arrivals. China uses a multi-pronged approach to amplify its soft power, besides the Shanghai Expo and Beijing Olympics[237]. Moreover, China has emerged as a major foreign aid donor with much influence[238]. India to assert its international presence in the past decade has increased its foreign aid to countries in Africa and Asia in several projects such as energy, agriculture and infrastructure[239].

Furthermore, coinciding with the 'Make in India' initiative, the CCP has undertaken a 'Made in China' that will facilitate Research and Development (R&D) to further elevate 'Made in China as per the CCP[240]. Also, importantly, the problem of the ageing population in China is due to the "One-child policy". According to the Chinese Academy of Social Sciences study, China's population will peak in 2029 before entering a declining state and by 2065 it will return to the levels of the mid-1990s, which will rapidly slow the economic growth[241]. In contrast, India is said to have the largest working-age population by 2050 which offers numerous and attractive opportunities for the future of India[242].

Nye stated that the "best propaganda is no propaganda"[243]. In this context, even as China spends billions, the U.S spends millions and regardless one sees how people globally including Indians are dreaming and thinking of America[244]. Shambaugh, an American scholar asserted that China conducts a transactional manner of diplomacy, carefully considering national benefits and costs instead of contributing to the global share of "public goods" where China punches way below its weight. China may be ahead of India in "hard power" yet when it comes to soft power, India could be ahead of China[245]. India and China have been at crossroads and recognition of India's multilateral aspirations by China are overdue[246]. There may be abundant scope for both countries to cooperate on a spectrum of problems such as climate change, global health and emerging technologies[247].

4.5 The post-COVID World Soft Power: India and China

Several elements have pushed the fall of China's soft power for reasons such as the outbreak and spread of COVID-19, Chinese regional developments in Hong Kong and Xinjiang and the influence of the increasing US-China conflict[248]. China has been demonstrating a more proactive outlook and even belligerent methods of public communication, probably seeking at thwarting adverse criticism, instead of attaining attractiveness[249]. Lately, China's "hyper-aggressive diplomatic style" has backfired due to the use of its "Wolf warrior strategy", a diplomatic style that is innately undiplomatic, and aims to attack, abuse or confront nations when China is being questioned[250]. Thus, Chinese diplomacy has suffered enormously because of this strategy as the new generation diplomats have been instructed to defend China's atrocities on minorities, the mishandling of COVID and its hyper-militaristic foreign policy[251]. Furthermore, this could lead to a conflict between major powers and China's neighbors[252].

The experience of China shows that nation-branding approaches may not allow modifying the perception of the global society about the country[253]. The rise of China continues to cause anxiety and concern despite setting up 'CIs" globally to educate the community about Chinese civilization and language, making statements about China's peaceful rise, delivering foreign aid to many African nations, hosting the Summer Olympic Games and fostering economic and cultural ties across Asia through BRI[254]. Additionally, the 'Made in China' label does not encourage much trust among consumers due to questions concerning product source and quality[255]. An authoritative governmental system, a muscular foreign policy and increasing political and economic aims have caused discontent in several parts globally[256]. Whereas, India's PD desires to persuade the world that it is unlikely to engage in armed or economic disputes and is barely a danger to the international community as the largest democracy in the world, being the birthplace of Gandhi and Buddha who showcased the non-violent temperament, the declaration of no first use of its nuclear weapons, underlining pluralism and tolerance[257].

Though India seeks to be a rising power it does not strive to export its political system or economic ideology to other nations as it aims to be incorporated into the international system on the power of its soft power and economic accomplishments, rather than military abilities[258]. Also, the pace of India's rising power status is gradual compared to China and will allow the global society time to adapt to India's rise[259]. India believes that it can reform the present IOs to provide a more important role to itself and other nations in the developing world[260]. India's position is also supported by the view that it is unlikely to be hostile towards the west as it neither showcases a robust sense of historical grievance against the west nor is it impacted by strong anti-west within its politic frame[261]. India's goal is to provide that established powers will not embrace obstructionist standings under the facade of its rising aspirations[262]. Today, the image of a country is significant in a world where rising powers are treated with concern and anxiety, and competition for tourism, commerce and investment is acute[263]. Pew Research 2018 Global Attitudes Survey indicates that survey in the Asia-Pacific region nations held favorable views towards India[264]. A following survey among western nations also states that India performs a more significant role globally today as compared to a decade ago[265].

The PD of China of similar to that of India but the way it projects its nation-branding is due to its Communist political system unlike the democratic political system of India. Also, the powerful top-down strategy is characteristic of Chinese soft power initiatives, meeting with little success despite enormous expenditures[266]. Post-COVID, China has continued its actions to fortify its position in International Institutions, mainly within the specialized agencies of the U.N[267]. China wants to construct standards, norms, regulations and rules that would facilitate their long-term strategy and weaken the U.S International standing[268]. The increasing leverage of China in global institutions is also due to the isolationist movements of the U.S[269].

China has also increased its interest in the Arctic and Antarctica region through the Polar Silk Road, which is part of BRI[270]. These two regions are also part of the country's expanding foreign policies where China wants to be recognized by the international community as a stakeholder[271]. CCP also has ambitions to build China into a "polar great power" by 2030[272]. In the recent times, China has been using the "salami-slicing strategy" that involves making small and incremental encroachments into India's territory that don't escalate into war but put together give China a strategic advantage[273]. China has been using this strategy in several places including SCS[274]. Similarly, as per a top foreign policy think tank, China has begun to dominate the U.N and control many U.N bodies[275]. Thus, to balance it, India should strive to play a proactive role.[276] However, post the Galwan incident, GOI has banned several Chinese apps besides removing the Chinese language from the curriculum of Indian schools[277].

The literature on the rise of great powers including China's rise, in particular, is broadly diverged into "power transition theory", the realist camp that includes defensive and offensive realism besides the liberal school of thought[278]. The power transition theory is seen by scholars to examine the rise of China and envision a future where significant disputes and warfare is unavoidable[279]. Power transition theory envisions dispute as a consequence of a rising power contending with a predominant power where the former seeks to revamp the rules of the system and institution by force, if required, to alter the status quo[280]. Scholars such as Mearsheimer through the theory of offensive realism, indicate that aggressive, expansionist and hegemonic conduct would characterize China's rise[281]. Recently, through "Mask Diplomacy" post-COVID, China's global reputation has also been mixed due to backlash from several countries[282]. China, as a $10 trillion economy with increasing military power and border confrontations with many of its neighbors, its hard power usually works to undermine its soft power[283]. Challenges such as the overcapacity of state-owned enterprises, environmental pollution and degradation, the sweeping anti-corruption campaigns Xi, food security problems and the overcapacity of state-owned enterprises are presumably to discourage others from pursuing China's model[284].

A healthy civil society represents creating actual ideas, art and expression and the blooming of soft power[285]. Also, the state can strengthen an independent civil society that enables for blooming of soft power[286]. Nye stated that "the best propaganda is not propaganda" where there should be a two-way relationship between civil society and the state[287]. As per Nye, civil society needs to have enough autonomy and freedom from the state to build its ideas for the world to follow[288]. In China's context, the top-down approach requires to be backed by a bottom-up approach that supports the growth of the country's soft power[289]. To enhance its soft power, China should maintain calm and silence and not respond to evocative public comments from the west. This could likewise help China construct its global benevolence[290].

American Political Scientist, Samuel Huntington in the book "The Clash of Civilizations and the Remaking of World Order" states that the rise of China and the growing assertiveness of this largest player in the early 21st century will create enormous anxiety about the global stability[291]. Nevertheless, post-COVID, unlike China, India has been shaping a 'new multilateralism' as the country is qualified to perform a leadership role in the present global order[292]. India, known as the "Pharmacy of the world" for the last two decades has been supplying affordable medicines conforming to quality standards to international markets. GOI announced an elaborate "vaccine diplomacy" strategy for providing vaccines to several countries[293].

4.6 Conclusion

Forecasts that the 21st century will be known as the "Asian century" have been made for years where Asia and the world have undergone dramatic circumstances and metamorphosis[294]. Asia has been attracting more global attention due to its exceptional strength with many ups and downs and primarily because the significance of Asia in IR continues to expand[295]. Today, India's rise, unlike the rise of China, is not being considered with apprehension and anxiety in several nations[296]. Presently, Asia may become the most critical laboratory for the subsequent stage of power in IR. India and China should recognize the necessity for a multipolar Asia and demonstrate a growing desire in delivering collective goods in the global arena and share accountabilities. Hymans states how Nye considers the liberal democratic system of India as a true edge over China in the two Asian giants' competition for international influence and attractiveness.

Martin Jacques, a British journalist and author of "When China Rules the World: The End of the Western World and the Birth of a New World Order" has put forth the emergence of China as the next superpower[297]. Though the U.S stays the exclusive superpower while with the elevation, notably China, the current form of the global order will ultimately be reconfigured[298]. Though given these challenges, China has a lengthy and complex route forward before it can claim the position of a superpower[299]. Also, for China to achieve hegemonic standing in the global setting it must correspondingly become an innovative society that fosters political and economic establishments[300]. As the CCP celebrates the centenary of its founding in 2049, it hopes to be a "world power" where the country's rapid military modernization, and expanding economic and diplomatic influence are all part of this goal. However, in the India and China soft power ties, there should be a constructive bilateral engagement and the spirit of growing together in 'cooperative engagement'.

Notes

1. Albert, et.al (2021) *The Chinese Communist Party*. Available at: https://www.cfr.org/backgrounder/chinese-communist-party (Accessed 12 January 2022)
2. Wu (2013) 'When the sleeping dragon dreams', *CPD blog*, 23 May, Available at: https://uscpublicdiplomacy.org/blog/when-%E2%80%9Csleeping-dragon%E2%80%9D-dreams (Accessed 2 February 2022)
3. *Ibid.*
4. *Ibid.*
5. Yang, Y (2017) *China's Communist party raises army of nationalist trolls*. Available at: https://www.ft.com/content/9ef9f592-e2bd-11e7-97e2-916d4fbac0da (Accessed: 4 February 2022)

6 *Ibid.*

7. Sandhu (2011) *China's Quest for Global Dominance: Reality or Myth.* New Delhi: United Services Institution.

8. Ambrosetti (2012) *Power and influence: Ideational and material factors in the International posture of China rising as a great power,* Doctoral thesis, Georgetown university, viewed 12 February 2021, https://repository.library.georgetown.edu/bitstream/handle/10822/557678/Ambrosetti_georgetown_0076D_11857.pdf?sequence=1&isAllowed=y

9. *Ibid.*

10. *Ibid.*

11. *Ibid.*

12. *Ibid.*

13. *Ibid.*

14. *Ibid.*

15. *Asian century: Cooperation or conflict?* (2010). Available at: https://economictimes.indiatimes.com/opinion/et-commentary/asian-century-cooperation-or-conflict/articleshow/6208284.cms?from=mdr (Accessed: 23 February, 2022).

16. *Ibid.*

17. *Ibid.*

18. Kong, L. (2019) *Exploring China's Soft Power: Manifestations of the Chinese Dream in Contemporary Practices of Cultural Diplomacy.* PhD thesis, University of York, viewed 24 February 2020, Available at: https://etheses.whiterose.ac.uk/27062/7/Kong_202046173_Final%20Thesis%20revised%20.pdf

19. Palit. (2014) China's Cultural Diplomacy: Historical Origin, Modern Methods and Strategic Outcomes, *China Research Centre*, Vol. 12, No. 2.

20. *Ibid.*

21. Lim, L (2021) *Sticks and Stones: Realism, Constructivism, Rhetoric a great power Competition.* Available at: https://mwi.usma.edu/sticks-and-stones-realism-constructivism-rhetoric-and-great-power-competition/ (Accessed: 21 February 2022)

22. *Ibid.*

23. Kurlantzick, J (2006) China's Charm: Implications of Chinese Soft Power, *Carnegie Endowment Policy Brief*, No. 47, p. 1.

24. *Ibid.*

25. MacDonald (2015) *Analyzing China's rise in International relations theory: liberal institutionalism Part 3.* Available at: https://cdainstitute.ca/analyzing-china-s-rise-in-international-relations-theory-liberal-institutionalism-part-3/. (Accessed: 12 February 2022)

26. *Ibid.*

27. Sibley, G. M. (2013). *Literature Review: China through the Lens of Realism.* Nighhawks. Available at: https://digitalcommons.northgeorgia.edu (Accessed: 14 February 2022)

28. Freundlieb, M (2019) *A Constructivist Approach to Chinese Interest Formation in the South China Sea.* Available at: https://www.e-ir.info/2019/02/02/a-constructivist-approach-to-chinese-interest-formation-in-the-south-china-sea/ (Accessed: 17 February 2022)

29. *Ibid.*
30. *Ibid.*
31. Stewart, R. K (2018) *Strategic Puzzle in the South China Sea: Perception, power, and Money Chinese Plans for Hegemony?* Available at: https://sound-ideas.pugetsound.edu/cgi/viewcontent.cgi?article= 1023&context= ipe_theses (Accessed: 19 February 2022)
32. Aslan (2010) Soft power concept in the Chinese context, Master thesis, Middle East Technical University, Ankara, Viewed 23 February 2022, https://etd.lib.metu.edu.tr/upload/3/12611710/index.pdf
33. *Ibid.*
34. *Ibid.*
35. Miller (2017) *China's soft power: Can China make the grade?*. Available at http://public.wartburg.edu/mpsurc/images/JMiller.pdf
36. *Ibid.*
37. *Ibid.*
38. *Ibid.*
39. *Ibid.*
40. *Ibid.*
41. Mirza, et.al (2020) Evaluating China's Soft Power Discourse: Assumptions, Strategies, and Objectives, *Global Strategic & Security Studies Review*, ISSN: 2708-2121). 5. 40-50. 10.31703/gsssr.2020(V-IV).05.
42. Olson,Prestowitz (2011) The Evolving Role of China in International Institutions, *The U.S.-China* Economic and Security Review Commission: The Economic *Strategy Institute.* Available at: https://www.uscc.gov/sites/default/files/Research/TheEvolvingRoleofChinainInternationalInstitutions.pdf
43. *Ibid.*
44. *Ibid.*
45. Palit (2017) *Analyzing China's soft power strategy and comparative Indian initiatives.* New Delhi: SAGE
46. *Ibid.*
47. *Ibid.*
48. *Ibid.*
49. *Ibid.*
50. *Ibid.*
51. *Ibid.*
52. *Ibid.*
53. *Ibid.*
54. Huang, C.H (2013) *China's So Power in East Asia: A Quest for Status and Influence*, NBR Special Report No 42, viewed 12 February 2022, National Bureau of Asian Research.
55. *Ibid.*
56. *Ibid.*

57. Jamison, B (2021) A Constructivist Approach to a Rising China, *Journal of Indo-Pacific Affairs,* viewed 7 February 2022, Air University Press
58. *Ibid.*
59. *Ibid.*
60. *Ibid.*
61. *Ibid.*
62. Kuhn, F (2021) *Offensive Realism and the Rise of China: A Useful Framework for Analysis.* Available at: https://www.e-ir.info/2021/07/09/offensive-realism-and-the-rise-of-china-a-useful-framework-for-analysis/ (Accessed: 26 February 2022)
63. *Ibid.*
64. *Ibid.*
65. *Ibid.*
66. Hudda, N (215) *Interpreting the Rise of China: Realist and Liberalist Perspectives*. Available at: https://www.e-ir.info/2015/04/03/interpreting-the-rise-of-china-realist-and-liberalist-perspectives/(Accessed: 24 February 2022)
67. *Ibid.*
68. Zhang, Austin (2014) Power and Responsibility in Chinese Foreign Policy, *ANU Press*, DOI: 10.22459/PRCFP.01.2014.
69. *Ibid.*
70. Qin, Y. (2011). Development of International Relations Theory in China: Progress through Debates. *International Relations of the Asia-Pacific*. 11. 231-257. 10.1093/irap/lcr003.
71. *Ibid.*
72. *Ibid.*
73. DeLisle, J. (2010). Soft Power in a Hard Place: China, Taiwan, Cross-Strait Relations and U.S. Policy. *Orbis*. 54. 493-524. 10.1016/j.orbis.2010.07.002.
74. Joshi, M (2021) *China's attempt to redefine democracy*. Available at https://www.orfonline.org/expert-speak/chinas-attempt-to-redefine-democracy/ (Accessed: 3 January 2022)
75. *Ibid.*
76. Kong, L (2019) *Exploring China's Soft Power: Manifestations of the Chinese Dream in Contemporary Practices of Cultural Diplomacy.* PhD thesis, University of York, viewed 9 February 2022, https://etheses.whiterose.ac.uk/27062/7/Kong_202046173_Final%20Thesis%20revised%20.pdf
77. *Ibid.*
78. Weisser, P (2019) The Soft Power Practices of the Ming Dynasty and Zheng He's First Voyage, *History in the Making*: Vol. 12, Article 9.
79. *Ibid.*
80. *Ibid.*
81. *Ibid.*
82. *Ibid.*

83. Shen (2020) *The World Is Awakening to China's Sharp Power*. Available at: https://thediplomat.com/2020/06/the-world-is-awakening-to-chinas-sharp-power/ (Accessed: 15 February 2022)
84. *Ibid.*
85. Yuan, L (2019) *China's Soft-Power Failure: Condemning Hong Kong's Protests.* Available at: https://www.nytimes.com/2019/08/20/business/china-hong-kong-social-media-soft-power.html (Accessed: 18 February 2022)
86. *Ibid.*
87. *Ibid.*
88. Meng, M. (2012) Chinese Soft Power: The Role of Culture and Confucianism, Syracuse University, *Honors Program Capstone Projects*. 182.
89. *Ibid.*
90. Sukheja, B (2021) China Channelizes Ideologies To Defame Democracy, Promote Authoritarian Governance: Report. Available at: https://www.republicworld.com/world-news/china/china-Channelises-ideologies-to-defame-democracy-promote-authoritarian-governance-report.html (Accessed: 16 February 2022).
91. Hamilton, D (2016) *Checkbook Diplomacy*. Available at: https://archive.transatlanticrelations.org/publication/checkbook-diplomacy-daniel-s-hamilton/ (Accessed: 18 February 2022)
92. *Ibid.*
93. Sharma, Lin (2021). Does China engage in debt-trap diplomacy? *IPS Working Paper Series No.*1. Hong Kong: Institute of Policy Studies, Lingnan University. DOI: 10.14793/ipswp2021001
94. *Ibid.*
95. *Ibid.*
96. *Ibid.*
97. *Ibid.*
98. *Ibid.*
99. Chaudhury, S.R (2021) *How China is Expanding Global Influence via Debt Trap Diplomacy*. Available at: https://thewire.in/world/china-debt-trap-diplomacy-south-asia-europe (Accessed: 19 February 2022)
100. Gupta, S (2022) Chinese loans for white elephant projects pushed SL and Pak into present crisis. Available at: https://www.hindustantimes.com/world-news/chinese-loans-for-white-elephant-Projects-pushed-sl-and-pak-into-present-crisis-101649128210464.html (Accessed: 2 May 2022)
101. Rajah, et.al (2019) Ocean of debt: Belt and Road and debt diplomacy in the Pacific, *Lowy Institute for international policy*. http://hdl.handle.net/11540/11721.
102. *Ibid.*
103. Das, D (2022) *China's 'debt-trap Diplomacy' Fuels Sri Lanka's Foreign Exchange Crisis: Report*. Available at: https://www.republicworld.com/world-news/rest-of-the-world-news/chinas-debt-trap-Diplomacy-fuels-sri-lankas-foreign-exchange-crisis-report-articleshow.html (Accessed: 19 February 2022)

104. Were, A. (2018) *Debt trap: Chinese loans and Africa's development options*. Available at https://saiia.org.za/research/debt-trap-chinese-loans-and-africas-development-options/ (Accessed: 9 February 2022)

105. *Ibid.*

106. Lloyd, Felstead (2013) A Chinese Scramble for Africa? To what extent does China acts as a neo-colonialist on the African continent. *Lund University.*

107. Chaudhury (2021) *Africa's rising debt: Chinese loans to continent exceeds $140 billion.* Available at: https://m.economictimes.com/news/international/world-news/africas-Rising-debt-chinese-loans-to-continent-exceeds-140-billion/articleshow/86444602.cms (Accessed: 16 February 2022)

108. Jones, H. (2020) Debunking the Myth of 'Debt-trap Diplomacy: How Recipient Countries Shape China's Belt and Road Initiative. *Asia-Pacific Programme Chatham House.* Circa 44 Seiten

109. Scott, J (2019), *Chinese spies spook democracies from US to Europe to Australia.* Available at: https://economictimes.indiatimes.com/news/defence/chinese-spies-spook-democracies-from-u-s-to-Europe-to-australia/articleshow/72239308.cms?From=mdr. (Accessed: 12 February 2022)

110. Silver, et.al (2020) *Unfavorable Views of China Reach Historic Highs in Many Countries*. Available at: https://www.pewresearch.org/global/2020/10/06/unfavorable-views-of-china-reach-historic-highs-in-many-countries/. (Accessed: 12 February 2022)

111. Yuen, S.(2015). Friend or Foe: The Diminishing Space of China's Civil Society. *China Perspectives.* 2015. 51-56. DOI: 10.4000/chinaperspectives.6807.

112. Gleiss, et. al (2018). Re-theorizing civil society in China: Agency and the discursive politics of civil society engagement. *China Information.33*, 22 - 3.

113. *Ibid.*

114. *Ibid.*

115. Inboden, R. (2021). China at the UN: Choking Civil Society. *Journal of Democracy*, *32*(3), 124-35.

116. *Ibid.*

117. *Ibid.*

118. *Ibid.*

119. *China passes new laws on foreign NGOs amid international criticism* (2016). Available at: https://www.bbc.com/news/world-asia-china-36157052 (Accessed: 18 February 2022)

120. Herr, R. (2019). The yin and yang of soft power. In Chinese influence in the Pacific Islands: The yin and yang of soft power. *Australian Strategic Policy Institute.* pp. 12–14.

121. *Ibid.*

122. *Confucius Institutes 'just the tip of the iceberg' of China's sharp power* (2019). Available at: https://www.demdigest.org/confucius-institutes-just-the-tip-of-the-iceberg-of-chinas-sharp-power/

123. Jhakar, P. (2019) Confucius Institutes: The growth of China's controversial cultural branch. Available at: https://www.bbc.com/news/world-asia-china-49511231 (Accessed: 13 February 2022)

124. Venkataraman, P (2020) *China's Soft Power: Why Confucius Institutes Are Under Scrutiny in India and Across the Globe.* Available at: https://www.news18.com/news/india/chinas-soft-power-why-confucius-institutes-are-under-scrutiny-in-india-and-across-the-globe-2796907.html (Accessed: 19 February 2022)
125. *China: Crimes Against Humanity in Xinjiang (2021).* Available at: https://www.hrw.org/news/2021/04/19/china-crimes-against-humanity-xinjiang (Accessed: 23 December 2021)
126. Craig, V (2018) *Realism and Cyber Conflict: Security in the Digital Age*. Available at: https://www.e-ir.info/2018/02/03/realism-and-cyber-conflict-security-in-the-digital-age/(Accessed: 3 March 2022)
127. *Ibid.*
128. Brar, A (2021) *China's cyber warfare has grown on the back of civilian recruits.* Available at: https://theprint.in/opinion/eye-on-china/chinas-cyber-warfare-has-grown-on-the-back-of-civilian- Recruits/737651/ (Accessed: February 23 2022)
129. *Ibid.*
130. *Ibid.*
131. *Ibid.*
132. *Ibid.*
133. Park. (2019) *The global failure of cinematic soft power 'with Chinese characteristics*. Available at: https://theasiadialogue.com/2019/05/27/the-global-failure-of-cinematic-soft-power-with-chinese-Characteristics/ (Accessed: 14 March 2022)
134. *Ibid.*
135. *Ibid.*
136. Feng (no date). *The silver and white economy: The Chinese demographic challenge*. Available at: https://www.oecd.org/employment/leed/OECD-China-report-Final.pdf (Accessed: 28 March 2022)
137. Saeed (2015) *China's soft power: changing the world perception,* Master thesis, Monterey, California: Naval Postgraduate School, viewed 13 February, https://1library.net/document/q54n8mjy-china-s-soft-power-changing-the-world-perception.html
138. *Ibid.*
139. *Ibid.*
140. *Ibid.*
141. *Ibid.*
142. Kurnosenko. (2010) *China, the Dalai Lama and the Question of Soft Power*, Master thesis, Central European University, Viewed 12 February 2022, kurnosenko_ekaterina.pdf
143. *Ibid.*
144. *Ibid.*
145. *Ibid.*
146. Whyte, A. (2013) *Interpreting the Rise of China.* Available at: https://www.e ir.info/2013/02/13/interpreting-the-rise-of-china/ (Accessed: 18 February 2022)

147. Rowthorn, R (2007) *The Renaissance of China and India: Implications for the Advanced Economics.* Available at: https://unctad.org/system/files/official-document/osgdp20071_en.pdf (Accessed: 23 February 2022)
148. *Ibid.*
149. Muni. (No date) *India, China and the Asian Century.* Jawaharlal Nehru University.
150. *Ibid.*
151. *Ibid.*
152. Mitra, A. (2021) *Comparative Analysis of India and China's Soft Power Diplomacy.* Available at: https://www.claws.in/comparative-analysis-of-india-and-chinas-soft-power-diplomacy/ (Accessed: 14 February 2022)
153. *Ibid.*
154. *Ibid.*
155. *Ibid.*
156. *Ibid.*
157. *Ibid.*
158. Caminati, D. (2018) *The 'Exceptional' Chinese Soft Power: Outlier or Pioneer?.* Available at: https://www.e-ir.info/2018/12/11/the-exceptional-chinese-soft-power-outlier-or-pioneer/(Accessed: 17 February 2022)
159. *Ibid.*
160. *Ibid.*
161. *Ibid.*
162. Karnik, K (2011) *India has enough clout to emerge a winner in global power.* Available at: https://economictimes.indiatimes.com/opinion/et-commentary/india-has-enough-clout-to-emerge-a-winner-in-global-power/articleshow/7870531.cms (Accessed: 12 February 2022)
163. *Ibid.* Amaresh, P (2020) India's Soft Power in the Line of Actual Control (LAC), Available at: https://diplomatist.com/2020/07/29/indias-soft-power-in-the-line-of-actual-control-lac/ (Accessed: 17 February 2022)
164. *Ibid.*
165. Dellios. (2000) China and India: New Mandalas of Power in 21st Century Geopolitics, *Essays on Development issues: India and the Indian Ocean region* (pp. 93-113), Atlantic.
166. *Ibid.*
167. Hunter, A (2009) Soft Power: China on the Global Stage, *The Chinese Journal of International Politics*, Volume 2, Issue 3, Pages 373–398. DOI: 10.1093/cjip/pop001.
168. *Ibid.*
169. Schmidt, J. (2020). Introduction: India and China in Comparative Perspective, *Emerging Asian and Global Powers.* 10.1007/978-3-030-44425-9_1.
170. *Ibid.*
171. *Ibid.*
172. *Ibid.*
173. *Ibid.*

174. *Ibid.*
175. *Ibid.*
176. Palit. (2010) China's soft power in South Asia. *RSIS working paper: No. 200.* Singapore: Nanyang Technological University.
177. *Ibid.*
178. *Ibid.*
179. Kent, A. (2014). China's participation in international organizations. 10.22459/PRCFP.01.2014.06.
180. *Ibid.*
181. *Ibid.*
182. Palit (2017) *Analyzing China's soft power strategy and Comparative Indian initiatives*. New Delhi: SAGE
183. *Ibid.*
184. Palit, Palit. (2011) Strategic Influence of Soft Power: Inferences for India from, Chinese Engagement of South and Southeast Asia. *-ICRIER, Policy Series*, No. 3.
185. *Ibid.*
186. *Ibid.*
187. *Ibid.*
188. *Ibid.*
189. *Ibid.*
190. Dutta, S. (2011) Managing and Engaging Rising China: India's Evolving Posture, *The Washington Quarterly*, 34:2, 127-144, DOI: 10.1080/0163660X.2011.564555.
191. Ahlawat, Hughes (2018) India–China Stand-off in Doklam: Aligning Realism with National Characteristics, *The Round Table,* 107:5, 613-625, DOI: 10.1080/00358533.2018.1530376.
192. *Ibid.*
193. *Ibid.*
194. *Ibid.*
195. *Ibid.*
196. *Ibid.*
197. Narayanan, R (2013) China and India: A Sisyphean Bilateral, *Policy Brief*, Rajaratnam School of International Studies.
198. *Ibid.*
199. Sharma, et.al (2021) Reflection of India-China Relations in Indian Media: Problems and Perspectives, *RUDN Journal of Studies in Literature and Journalism*. Vol. 26. N: 1, P. 142-148. DOI: 10.22363/2312-9220-2021-26-1-142-148.
200. *Ibid.*
201. Yasin (2020) Nation Branding and Public Diplomacy: India and China Compared, *Occasional Paper* 64, ICS.

202. *Ibid.*

203. Rao. (2022) *The Case for Harnessing Soft Power, or Why India Cannot Be Insular.* Available at: https://thewire.in/diplomacy/india-soft-power-nirupama-rao (Accessed: 23 February 2022)

204. *Ibid.*

205. *Ibid.*

206. *Ibid.*

207. DNA(2021) *WION takes giant strides, marks its presence in 190 countries worldwide*. Available at: https://www.dnaindia.com/india/report-wion-takes-giant-strides-marks-its-presence-in-190-countries-worldwide-2875629 (Accessed: 25 February 2022)

208. Reuters (2016) *China's CCTV launches global 'soft power' network to extend influence.* Available at: https://fortune.com/2016/12/31/chinas-cctv-global-influence/ (Accessed: 23 February 2022)

209. PTI. (2016) *Tap 'positive energies' in Sino-India ties: China to media*. Available at: https://www.indiatoday.in/pti-feed/story/tap-positive-energies-in-sino-india-ties-china-to-media-715543-2016-10-13 (Accessed: 23 February 2022)

210. PTI (2015) *Sushma Swaraj highlights the role of media in promoting Sino-India ties*. Available at: https://economictimes.indiatimes.com/news/politics-and-nation/sushma-swaraj-highlights-role-of-Media-in-promoting-Sino-India-ties/articleshow/46084976.cms (Accessed: 12 February 2022)

211. *Ibid.*

212. Bandurski (no date) *Public Diplomacy*. Available at: https://decodingchina.eu/public-diplomacy/ (Accessed: 23 February 2022)

213. *Ibid.*

214. *Ibid.*

215. *Ibid.*

216. Liu, T, Song, Y. (2020) Chinese Para-diplomacy: A theoretical Review, *SAGE Open*. DOI: 10.1177/2158244019899048.

217. *Ibid.*

218. Amaresh, P (2020). *Diplomacy within Diplomacy: The Upswing of Para Diplomacy in India.* Available at: https://diplomatist.com/2020/06/01/diplomacy-within-diplomacy-the-upswing-of-Para-diplomacy-in-India/ (Accessed: 23 February 2022)

219. Bhonsle (2019) Religious tourism as soft power: Strengthening India's outreach to Southeast Asia, *ORF special report no 97,* Observer Research Foundation.

220. Know India Programme, Ministry of External Affairs. Available at: https://www.mea.gov.in/know-India-programme.htm (Accessed: 22 February 2022)

221. Zhu. (2007). Two Diasporas: Overseas Chinese and Non-resident Indians in Their Homelands' Political Economy. *Journal of Chinese Political Science*. 12. 281-296. DOI: 10.1007/s11366-007-9012-4.

222. *Ibid.*

223. *Ibid.*

224. Financial Express (2018) *Why pushing Hindi at UN an expression of India's soft power, not Chauvinism*. Available at: https://www.financialexpress.com/opinion/why-pushing-hindi-at-un-an-Expression-of-India's-soft-power-not-chauvinism/1008718/ (Accessed: 23 February 2022)

225. *Ibid.*

226. *Ibid.*

227. Menon, N. (2019) *India's history of elephant diplomacy.* Available at: https://caravanmagazine.in/lede/india-history-elephant-diplomacy (Accessed: 23 February 2022)

228. PTI. (2016) *Delhi zoo bats for animal diplomacy*. Available at: https://timesofindia.indiatimes.com/home/environment/delhi-zoo-bats-for-animal-Diplomacy/articleshow/53582484.cms (Accessed: 27 February 2022)

229. *Ibid.*

230. *Amaresh, P (2018) Fluffy Ambassadors: China's Panda Diplomacy*, ICS blog, 16 January, Available at: https://icsin.org/blogs/2018/01/16/fluffy-ambassadors-chinas-panda-diplomacy/(Accessed: 12 February 2022)

231. *Ibid.*

232. *Ibid.*

233. FP (2022) *China marks 50 years of 'panda diplomacy' with U.S: How Beijing used animal to push Agenda.* Available at: https://www.firstpost.com/world/china-marks-50-years-of-panda-diplomacy-With-us-how-beijing-used-animal-to-push-agenda-10376671.html (Accessed: 18 February 2022)

234. Chaziza, M (2019) *China's Outbound Tourism as a Soft Power Tool in the Middle East.* Available At: https://www.mei.edu/publications/chinas-outbound-tourism-soft-power-tool-middle-east (Accessed: 8 March 2022)

235. *Ibid.*

236. *Ibid.*

237. Dalmia, V (2018) *Will China succeed in its soft power strategy*?. Available at: https://www.orfonline.org/expert-speak/43982-will-china-succeed-in-its-soft-power-strategy/(Accessed: 5 March 2022)

238. Haibing. Z (no date) *The Development and Transformation of China's Foreign Aid*, CSIS, viewed 3 March 2022, CSIS, Washington D.C

239. *Schulz, M (no date)* India's foreign aid explained, Borgen Project, viewed 8 March 2021, Borgen Project

240. PTI. (2014) *'Made in China' campaign launched with 'Make in India'*. Available at: https://indianexpress.com/article/business/economy/made-in-china-campaign-launched-with-make-in-india/ (Accessed: 23 March 2022)

241. Campbell, C (2019) *China's Aging Population Is a Major Threat to Its Future.* Available at: https://time.com/5523805/china-aging-population-working-age/ (Accessed: 21 March 2022)

242. Pai, M (2011) *2050: India to have the largest working-age population*. Available at: https://economictimes.indiatimes.com/special-feature/2050-india-to-have-the-largest-working-age-population/articleshow/7388225.cms (Accessed: 23 March 2022)

243. Vishwanath, A (2017) *In 'soft power', China cuts no ice with India, but are such investments elsewhere paying dividends*. Available at: https://www.financialexpress.com/opinion/in-soft-power-china-cuts-no-ice-with-india-but-are-such-investments-elsewhere-paying-Dividends/620103/ (Accessed: 24 March 2022)

244. *Ibid.*

245. *Ibid.*

246. Gokhale, V. (2021) *The Road from Galwan: The Future of India-China Relations.* Available at: https://carnegieindia.org/2021/03/10/road-from-galwan-future-of-india-china-relations-pub-84019 (Accessed: 23 March 2022)

247. *Ibid.*

248. Dams, et.al (2021) China's Soft Power in Europe: Falling on Hard Times, *European Think-tank Network on China (ETNC)*, viewed 27 March 2021, Clingendael, The Netherlands

249. *Ibid.*

250. Pant, HV. (2021) *Is China backtracking on its wolf warrior diplomatic style?* Available at: https://www.orfonline.org/research/is-china-backtracking-on-its-wolf-warrior-diplomatic-style/(Accessed: 25 March 2022)

251. *Ibid.*

252. *Ibid.*

253. Mazumdar, A. (2020) 'India's Public Diplomacy in the Twenty-First Century: Components, Objectives and Challenges', *India Quarterly*, 76(1), pp. 24–39. DOI: 10.1177/0974928419901188.

254. *Ibid.*

255. *Ibid.*

256. *Ibid.*

257. *Ibid.*

258. *Ibid.*

259. *Ibid.*

260. *Ibid.*

261. *Ibid.*

262. *Ibid.*

263. *Ibid.*

264. *Ibid.*

265. *Ibid.*

266. Cutchin, J (2018) *How China is building its soft power: Pacific council on International policy.* Available at: https://www.pacificcouncil.org/newsroom/how-china-building-its-soft-power (Accessed: 28 March 2022)

267. Paszak. (2020) *China's growing Influence in International organizations.* Available at: https://warsawinstitute.org/chinas-growing-influence-international-organizations/ (Accessed: 29 March 2022)

268. *Ibid.*

269. *Ibid.*

270. Lanteigne. (2021) *The polar policies in China's new five-year plan*. Available at: https://thediplomat.com/2021/03/the-polar-policies-in-chinas-new-five-year-plan/ (Accessed: 12 March 2022)
271. *Ibid.*
272. Doshi, et.al (2021) *Northern expedition: China's Arctic activities and Ambitions*, Brookings, viewed 29 March 2022, Brookings, Washington D.C
273. Sitaraman, S. (2020) China's salami-slicing tactics and the latest India China border standoff, Security Nexus perspectives, Asia Pacific Centre for Security Studies.
274. *Ibid.*
275. Chaudhury, R (2021) *China dominates UN by controlling several UN bodies: Report*. Available at: https://economictimes.indiatimes.com/news/international/world-news/china-dominates-un-by-Controlling-several-un-bodies-report/articleshow/83080526.cms? From=mdr (Accessed: 2 April 2022).
276. *Ibid.*
277. Chaudhury, R (2020) *From visas to youth exchanges, govt weighs options to limit China's soft power in India*. Available at: https://economictimes.indiatimes.com/news/politics-and-nation/govt-Weighs-options-to-limit-chinas-soft-power-in-india/articleshow/77379977.cms (Accessed: 6 April 2022).
278. Jalil, G. Y. (2019) China's Rise: Offensive or Defensive Realism. *Strategic Studies*, *39*(1), 41–58.
279. *Ibid.*
280. *Ibid.*
281. *Ibid.*
282. Chen, Molter (2020) Mask Diplomacy: Chinese Narratives in the COVID Era, *Stanford blog*, Freeman Spogli Institute for International Studies, 16 June. Available at: https://fsi.stanford.edu/news/covid-mask-diplomacy.
283. Gracie, C (2015) *China power audit: The hard and the soft*. Available at: https://www.bbc.com/news/explainers-35100098 (Accessed: 12 April 2022).
284. Albert. (2018) *China's big bet on soft power.* Available at: https://www.cfr.org/backgrounder/chinas-big-bet-soft-power (Accessed: 11 April 2022).
285. Herbert, et.al (2021) China's Soft Power & Digital Trade: Reshaping Global Image Through Digital Media & Entertainment, *Working Paper Series,* Middlebury Institute of International Studies.
286. *Ibid.*
287. *Ibid.*
288. *Ibid.*
289. *Ibid.*
290. *Ibid.*
291. Nye, J (2020) Perspectives for a China Strategy, *PRISM*, Vol. 8, No. 4, National Defence University Press.
292. Spisbah (2020) *India is shaping a 'new multilateralism' in a post-COVID world*. Available at: https://melbourneasiareview.edu.au/india-is-shaping-a-new-multilateralism-in-a-post-covid-world/ (Accessed: 13 April 2022).

293. Dhar. (2021) *India's Vaccine Diplomacy*. Available at: https://www.globalpolicyjournal.com/blog/08/04/2021/indias-vaccine-diplomacy (Accessed: 14 April 2022)
294. Fidler (2005) The Asian Century: Implications for International law. Available at: https://www.repository.law.indiana.edu/cgi/viewcontent.cgi?Article=1397&context=facpub (Accessed: 16 April 2022)
295. *Ibid.*
296. Rithambara. (2013) *On Indian public diplomacy*. Available at: https://www.e-ir.info/2013/04/30/on-indian-public-diplomacy/ (Accessed: 18 April 2022)
297. Masoud (2014) Can China become the next superpower? *CPD blog*, Viewed 13 October, Available at: https://uscpublicdiplomacy.org/blog/can-china-become-next-superpower (Accessed: 19 April 2022)
298. *Ibid.*
299. *Ibid.*
300. *Ibid.*

Chapter Five

Epilogue: Filling the Gaps- Advancing India's Soft power in the 21st Century

5.1 The Gaps in India's Soft Power

Understanding and utilizing soft power to the advantage of the nation can therefore go a long way in improving ties between a nation and rest of the world. This book aims to address all these issues along the way and serve as a foundation over which future studies or research could be carried out on several aspects of India's soft power and the role of state and civil society in influencing soft power. Since soft power is perceived to be an intangible ingredient of a state's power, it is difficult to measure the definite impact of these measures. The soft power has likewise functioned independently of government policies without the backing of a focused policy or adequate backing with financial resources.

India's journey from being a socially unequal, poor nation following its independence has paved the way for a flourishing journey to become a major geopolitical and geo-economic actor within the enduring institutional framework of constitutional democracy. India is the largest secular democracy, a benign global and regional power because of its great strength as it is soon to become the third largest economy in the future and its soft power has held its moral authority in International discourse post-independence through several forms which has been looked with enthralling respect and ever growing inquisitiveness and with the notion of "Vasudhaiva Kutumbakam" (World is one family). Today, India has recognized the evolution of a new security structure through transformations in global power and as grounds of the international order seem shaken. The economic reforms of the 1990s have seen both civilizational and economic renaissance. Also, the struggles of the 19th century reformers had led India to an abundance of opinions. The country presently has a great and prosperous global diaspora that connects it through global linkages, which it had not experienced since the days of the ancient spice trade. The proactive and extensional diplomatic ambitions of India have led to a high-level engagement with several countries. Today, the constructivism of "Asian values" as a form of soft power is rising in Asia. Till date Asia's soft power initiatives have been more receptive in neighboring countries due to proximity, close cultural ties, trade relations and diaspora. This has comprehensively increased India's influence in foreign affairs.

Due to India's status as a global power, a consolidated democracy and a country, that is free from colonial influence, Indian foreign assistance has great legitimacy in the eyes of other emerging countries legitimacy, which is likely to bolster its soft power. Outside regional foreign and defense ministries, the 21st century Indian success story is so important for its soft-power credentials is still viewed as a speculative bet. Asia, one of the most majestic landmasses in the world has not only been undergoing increased economic development and expansion but is also imperiled to the pervasiveness of larger domestic frictions. However, in the struggle to win support around Asia, India has an important advantage over China. India cannot realize its potential in this area, however, unless it proves to the world that its days of economic and social stagnation are truly a thing of the past.

Furthermore, Soft power is ever winning and Indian diplomacy has started effectively using the fast growing digital mediums besides the importance of Indian diaspora, social media in making decisions in the domain of foreign relations and diplomacy; also PD in leveraging India's soft power including nation-branding, diaspora outreach, digital engagement, international broadcasting and international exchange programmes. This in turn has facilitated foreign aid, International trade, foreign investment, foreign tourist arrivals, bilateral and multilateral economic cooperation contributing to the country's economic prosperity and political stability. Nevertheless, besides other sectors, India's human capital and skill development needs to be improved, communicating a favorable image of the country in a digitally connected world involving both governmental and NGO actors.

Additionally, India has struggled to leverage that wealth into diplomatic gain partly because governments usually find it hard to utilize soft power, since soft power is a product of a society, not a state. But in India's case there are additional issues such as the tiny size of the Foreign Service, which struggles to keep up with routine diplomacy, and can't spend much time on PD or CD. Likewise, gaps such as what one might call India's high ideals comprising both government aspirations or declarations and bigger philosophical principles India is sometimes seen to represent, like acceptance of multiple religious traditions and the everyday realities of India, where social and economic development lags behind where it should be, poverty remains acute, education is patchy and sometimes very poor, and so on. Also, India could invest more in public and cultural diplomacy, and that might help boost its soft power. But in the end, India's soft power will only grow when India's economy grows and the quality of life improves for the average citizen – when India is seen to be a success. Similarly, the achievement of soft diplomacy relies upon India's standing. To leverage India's soft power, yoga and Ayurveda should be pushed emphatically. India moreover is unique in its problems, from its large population, colonial history, poverty levels and ideological divisions. Thus, voicing can enhance Indian diplomacy for the right in every matter of global concern as far as it can balance the domestic interest. India should consider updating its foreign policy according to the changing world.

India should further require investing in ICCR, enhancing sports, DD, CD and tourism that can support in improving the Tier-1 diplomacy. Continuous engagement and contact of Indian diaspora by the MEA, which is the largest source of remittance in the world, can also be used to strengthen the FOREX besides providing soft loans and financial aid to the African and Asian nations. Importantly, India also needs to establish similar ties with South and South-East Asian nations besides other major powers like the U.S. The Indian nationalism needs to be in synchronization with multilateralism so that the existing race of protectionism is not increased.

CSOs can further contribute and join in the effort by not only flagging the problematic issues to the state institutions but also promote redressal of grievances which will help in enhancing the impact of India's soft power diplomacy. Civil society has a crucial role to play and has an immense outreach. However, some NGOs and organizations have also reportedly played a disruptive role either due to their philosophy or to serve their originators interests, which do not find favor in the government. On the whole, civil society's contribution to India's soft power is multi-fold and multi-dimensional which has elevated as well derogated the image of India on the International arena. Civil society contribution in formulation of opinion abroad has likewise helped in creating situations for foreign nations to enhance their relations with India. For example of the U.S where the rising Indian diaspora and civil society groups necessitates increasing ties with India. Thus, civil societies reflect the image of the nation abroad thereby

India's values, opinions and ethics in this way have been reflected in foreign nations. Similarly, civil society influences business groups to initiate and develop ties with nations that suit their demands thereby improving the tier-2 as well as tier-3 diplomacy by use of soft power. Instances of increasing trade interactions with Saudi Arabia and UAE are examples where the civil society influences the diplomacy at tier-1 level by use of soft power.

Though civil society considered as the "third power" has been contributing, a lot more can be done only when they understand their own power and use it appropriately. However, using digital power in state-civil society could help improve the image of India. Drawbacks such as population, poverty, poor education not reaching every one (though its is changing), political parties and political system, the pseudo secularism, manipulation of caste system, linguistic differences and regional affiliations all stand in the way of the civil society to be effective in India. Also, post-citizenship bill issue, the civil society was antagonized enough to question the credibility of India as a secular nation. The status of J&K as a union territory has made the civil society to campaign against such move, which made the international arena including friendly nations like U.S and European Union question the democratic and federal principles that India holds.

People have faith in civil society than government, which can be used to make interaction between state and them. However, sometimes civil society has not been effective as it is against development activities in India and further instigates the people to protest against several issues such as power projects etc. which leads to law and order problems. By effectively addressing and managing the country's development issues, India can then provide leadership and guidance to other developing countries, through creating a model for sharing information and best practices. Track-2 diplomacy and other non-official vehicles of bilateral and multilateral engagement owe their success to the energy and commitment of civil society actors. Nevertheless, the GOI, for its part, needs to take civil society members into greater confidence by stepping out of the confines of ideology, partisan politics and polarizing opinion. The state thus needs to use civil society even more vigorously as an instrument of exercising its soft power. Also, NGOs' interactions between states have proved to be extremely useful in fostering relations between governments during official standstills.

Furthermore, since the last two decades MEA has been actively engaging with CSOs, especially universities and think tanks in tier 2 and tier 3 cities by holding lectures, seminars and even diplomatic meetings. Therefore, it is important to note that soft power and civil society are two sides of the same coin and each enriches the other. Presently, India is perceived with the GOI effectively regulating its authority advancement help program with the foundation of the DPA division under the MEA. It is essential to take note that while civil society and government collaboration have been the subject of broad scholasticism just as strategy work in the last two decades, the exact connection between the two has not gotten the consideration it merits from the GOI. In India the focal point of common society has to a great extent been on domestic issues and the area all in all is yet to characterize its terms of commitment with international strategy, a region all the more regularly as best left to government offices answerable for it. Debates between the DPA and civil society have reinforced the idea that civil society as a select few civil society leaders can convincingly represent a concept armed with the intellectual sensibilities that fulfill the vision of the government's perception of the sector. This no doubt is problematic, and deserves more attention from researchers as well as practitioners, as to why a certain concept on of civil society is more favorable in the context of development cooperation between countries. Also, at the International level, civil societies play an important role and take interest in the developmental, cultural initiatives of the country, which gives a new facelift to the country's soft power. Contemporary day soft power diplomacy is enhanced to a level where the exchanges have been taking place between civil societies, NGO's etc. For instance, MEA jointly with ORF think tank conducted "Raisina Dialogue" in Delhi. Nevertheless, the full potential of the Indian civil society is yet to be tapped for better state-civil society.

In the media context, today it is focusing more on delivering the breaking news without proper research and analysis that has led to the deterioration of authenticity of the news among the public. There is foul act of media taking cash or taking courtesies from the corporate houses, government, ideological groups or large association, to show good news about them that is turning into a typical practice in reporting. Therefore, Indian media should maintain transparency and must avoid devoting their valuable times to non-issues that are not necessarily in public interest. The press in India has been given unprecedented freedom compared to other emerging economies like Brazil and China due to its role identified in the development process. So, the press must understand this responsibility and provide constructive criticism of the issues and avoid going in the race for TRP, as sense is more important than sensation. It is also important to create awareness regarding the importance of diplomatic ties among Indians besides establishing the credibility of Indian media. India can create its own media platform rather than utilizing the outsider's platform, which can be achieved through the country's immense capability of National Information Centre that will boost India's "self-reliance" in an effective manner. The media regulation especially the social media needs to be strengthened without affecting the freedom of the media and effective measures should be adhered by the GOI to improve its rankings in the Press Freedom Index. Also, public mood is easily understood from the social media responses and that helps in taking or fine-tuning important decisions in the domain of diplomacy.

It is important for India to continue nurturing its democracy and resilience at the grassroots level so that the projection for its soft power becomes a continuing flow of goodwill. To leverage soft power, the GOI has launched a major program known as "Digital India" and the "Indian diaspora" is further considered the most successful diaspora and feels emotional connected with India and often project the Indian ethos and culture daily. Today, "Social media" known to be a new instrument in which digital communication is embedded, India has emerged as a major conveyor of the soft power. "Media", known to be the 4th pillar of democracy, its self-regulation and independence are of utmost importance. Therefore, "media mongering" is to be avoided and governments have to acknowledge the powerful and important role of media not only as a mouthpiece but a keeper of conscience.

Further considering the review of India's foreign policy, it is known to be a continuous process in a fast changing world and the pandemic has abruptly forced the review of geo-political and geo-economic equations. Post cold war, India's policy of NAM had already given way to multi-alignment. In the context of country's foreign service, presently, India has the smallest number of diplomats among major foreign services globally though it has been gradually expanding the cadre where the pace needs to pick up. India now has close to 200 embassies and consulates across the world but in the 21st century diplomats should become tech savvy besides improving gender balance. MEA should consider investing more in language, region and subject matter specialists. Enrichment of diplomats at the New, Emerging and Strategic Technologies (NEST) division in MEA, which empower the diplomats about strategic technologies, will aid more in Industrialization 4.0. Furthermore, making the SAARC active through India's participation will enrich the regional cooperation even as Indo-pacific region is gaining more strength in International arena. But, Multi-lateralism India further requires support in setting benevolent parameters in the conduct of IOs with likeminded democracies and countries where India needs to take up the leadership role in various International platforms.

Consequently, to leverage India's soft power through Indian foreign policy, GOI needs to create a peace loving image of India and use the powerful media to project that image where despite huge population and opportunistic neighbors influenced by China, India is continuing staying on course to be secular, providing best of education to every child, medical facilities with doctors of outstanding skill etc., to show the world that India is certainly a power to reckon with and indeed the best friendly partner that a country can have. Also, the Indian diaspora must take the responsibility to be known as the "ambassadors of India" that could help in the amelioration of the Indian foreign policy through soft power. Today, Indian diaspora occupying chief positions in private entities, IO's, political entities of other nations could contribute to forging better relations with India and help develop a win-win situation for both the nations. Formulation of a shared vision will further India's soft power capability and also increase the interaction among the states and people. Through India's enhancement in digital diplomacy, instant and personal replies to SOS messages and catering to the needs of Indians abroad has been a unique quality of the MEA. The #AsktheSpokesperson initiative on Twitter allows the public to question India's foreign policy and are replied by the official spokesperson thereby creating awareness. Additionally, Indian foreign policy should follow de-hyphenation policy such that bilateral relationship of two countries is not affected as a result of conflict with a third country.

India's soft power has performed its charm heretofore without much state backing. The MEA and ICCR is playing an important role to push India's soft power further, governments previously formed the Ministry of Overseas Indian Affairs and a PPD within the MEA to further increase cultural exchanges in support of official diplomatic engagements. Nonetheless, so far there's little evidence to present that India for all its many soft power advantages has made a mark in international public view, despite the present government's keenness on leveraging the country's several soft-power resources to its democratic spirit in the pathway of its interests. Today, the country is sure about projecting its past heritage along with its modern values onto the world stage while persistent measures are needed by India to flourish as an international soft power. Currently, there has been a crucial phase in the discussion on soft power's position in global politics but for the first time, a coherent step is underway to boost India's brand value overseas which is likely to have significant implications for the conduct of Indian diplomacy and a more comprehensive role of India in world politics in the subsequent years.

Post-COVID India's Soft power has furthermore gained an upper hand compared to China's soft power. Unlike China, India's soft power is built through trust, credibility and democracy. China has faced the wrath of global community as they view China as origin of COVID, which is considered the biggest catastrophe on human progress after World War II. Following this, India became a viable alternative for china with its vast manpower and vibrant industrial ecosystem. Countries may run behind China for money but they realize their mistake when they get into debt and lose sovereignty but the world always pats India's empowerment approach. India needs to reaffirm its commitment to a multi- cultural, multi-lingual, multi-religious nature of its society, besides showing liberalism and progressivism in brandishing its soft power without diluting its core agenda. India should conduct digital exhibitions at its embassies abroad and where local people throng. India's standing as a free and open civilization state that has much to offer the rest of the world has already been amplified in different areas following the outbreak of the pandemic. The contrast with China is too obvious to require explanation here. In the context of India and China soft power ties, there needs to be a further spirit of expanding collectively in 'cooperative engagement" and structural bilateral ties. Furthermore, India could enhance its soft power standing globally through a patient and reasoned approach to a reordering of the international system. Also, India's rise of soft power during the pandemic is how several NGOs were involved in providing food support and basic necessities to poor and older networks.

Soft Power has therefore moved from being an academic concept to a political buzzword, particularly in the context of China and India. It has come under immense spotlight in the recent COVID crisis, where the soft power of the countries was reflected in the respective government's abilities in the management of pandemic. The Indian medicinal knowledge system such as Ayurveda has been included in the clinical trials for COVID and ancient practices like yoga have gained wider recognition bolstering India's soft power in the global realm. Besides the labor migration issues, amidst the pandemic crisis the world has also recognized the importance of the traditional Indian greeting, "Namaste," and many personalities internationally were seen using this mode of greeting. However, many believe China would still emerge as a global champion from this crisis and the external propaganda efforts have been intensified to repair the damage, create a positive narrative and sell the China story to the world. But this is not a zero-sum game – just because China's image is bad doesn't mean that India's is good – both can be bad, in different ways, at the same time.

5.2 Accessing the Gaps and Way Forward

There have been several dynamic and policy shifts in the last few years that have reshaped India's opinions in the external world. The Indian democracy can demonstrate to be an extensive soft power means if it is leveraged properly. Nevertheless, India in this way necessitates fixing its democracy internally by concentrating on domestic corruption and disorder and its outer picture where India is viewed as an inside looking nation. India's soft power has experienced blemishes due to major quandaries such as deep-rooted corruption, red-tapism, poverty, and violence against women, hostility to business, pollution in urban areas, bureaucratic barriers, caste-discrimination, investment issues copulated with an absence of investment in CD and gender-inequality has made India fare poorly in the elements of national attraction. The disputes between societies and faiths, huge levels of corruption, and several other interrelated concerns remain to plague India's global representation. The Indian soft power is no longer limited to Bollywood or global icons like Mahatma Gandhi, its own identity as a developing country with an entrenched democracy and the rising economic growth rates make it an increasingly attractive development model for other developing countries. India has soft power attraction abroad among the developing countries where it has made a significant effort to burnish its partnership image. Yet, its engagement has at times lacked policy coherence and efficacy.

Besides, soft power by itself will not suffice in the absence of palpable economic and hard power. For instance, South East Asia and Africa may have strong strategic convergences with India and yet it is China's prowess that gives it a decisive edge. India has not articulated a clear grand strategy on soft power. Soft power is not exactly in consonance with this line of thinking. Soft power should be part of the "grand strategy matrix" of a nation state. The MEA needs to educate citizens on this front. India, in spite of having soft power resources, grapples to rise as a significant power on the world platform. The decoupling within India's soft power outreach and national policies is disorienting, that is making other nations to blink at India. The nation's degenerating political environment is engulfing the breath out of Indian diplomacy and expunging any concrete communication emanating from the country's soft power projection. Soft power can create a favorable attitude but it is not always guaranteed that the other nation would act favorably and it takes more time than hard power. Nevertheless, in case India aspires for further global admiration, it needs to win it by manifesting more comprehensive democratic engagement and responsibility. India is likewise, ineffectively utilizing its soft power means within the Indian diaspora and at the hearth. It is important to reinvigorate the nation's representation in order to ennoble the lost grandeur of India. Over centuries, and especially through the colonial era, India was inadequate to establish on its preceding enrichment to different communities and unfortunately, the Buddhist connection too faded. Many archeological sites and cultural museums are being left out or haven't been conserved across India. Sites like Sarnath, Bodh Gaya, and so on of interest to the Buddhism religion have not been handled with the reverence and attention they justify. India should enhance Buddhism by promoting the' transnational Buddhist circuit' to revive the richness of Buddhism. Furthermore, Buddhism, an outreach of the diaspora, yoga, movies, literature, the chronicle of non-violent activism all of these can certainly be GOI advantages but, only if they are harmonious with internal affairs of the country. The communal riots, farmer suicides, suppression of the minorities are some of the instances that have kept India in scrutiny in last few years.

Consequently, 'Strategic independence' or autonomy is very crucial for India and it rages at any faultfinding of its internal policies that is generally expected from a 'pompous' and 'stalwart nation'. The country to be acknowledged as an international power requires opening its enormous potential to be a Soft power. India's use of soft power has been checked through key constraints like insufficiency of resources, particularly in contrast to major powers like the U.S and China, and the absence of a precise strategy due to intrinsic incongruities of India.

In the health care arena, despite India being acknowledged as the 'Pharmacy of the world' and referred as the 'Numero-Uno', for being the largest producer of the generic medicines and possessing the world's largest health care scheme, 'Ayushman Bharat', alongside displaying its soft power of medical tourism including telemedicine, the country lacks a proper health care system. This was quite apparent during COVID crisis. The citizens are seen spending a lot on health care, there is a shortage of human capital (doctors and other medical staff), shortage of beds and out of the pocket expenditure despite the country implementing various schemes since many schemes. Also, there are numerous factors at play forcing what feels like an underperformance in the 'Soft Power 30' index for India such as the western bias that places India at a relative disadvantage as advanced economy nations hold a lead.

India's course substantiates the idea of different analysts that soft power is most influential when backed by hard power as per scholars Tharoor, Lee and Blarel. However, India rather remains in a transitory stage where its hard power is however to become dominant even regionally to the end where it can meaningfully portray its soft power to build a political setting facilitative to its global objectives. India's immediate challenge lies in achieving the attention, status, and recognition of international power, instead of combating any negative stance that its elevation may have constructed in other states. This honor is presumably to come exclusively when the country handles its internal crises and improvises a more collective foreign policy within the current international order. Likewise, India's elites have yet to decide what type of power their country will be as it persists to grow, and this uncertainty shows a feeling of absurdity in the account of India's vision to the world.

Presently, poorer countries in global institutions like the African and small island countries in the climate change negotiations are constantly hindered by India's quest for self-interest over the appeals of developing countries, and wealthy nations criticize India's reluctance to compromise on matters that might cede some basis to the developed world. At a more fundamental level, India's multiple social and political identities persist to clash with each other such as in the directives and ideas that India displays globally besides its policymaking. The outcome is confusion at the receiving end, inconsistent policy changes, and public distrust among its interlocutors is not considered facilitative to the effectual practice of the country's soft power. Though India's cultural resources are ample, its inner dynamics and foreign policy are not considered appealing adequately for states to want what India desires.

It is just as essential to set the plan and structure the circumstances in global politics to get others to change in certain cases. Therefore, soft power can aid a nation to establish a plan and transform the choices of other countries before they come to the bargaining platform. So, if soft power is to benefit its interests India must take measures to address its identity polarities and domestic impediments. Nevertheless, soft power has the prospect to bear the endeavors of Indian diplomacy, and this consideration should be followed as a vital pursuit. The GOI efforts presently have been insufficient, concentrating more on image creation than constructing long-term associations. Indian leaders should consider fixing the disparities that are known to exist in a population of more than a billion in a diverse country like India.

According to Morgenthau, India boasts of all the conventional features considered vital for a state to become a great power such as natural resources, geography, being one of the biggest economies, industrial power, population with a considerable and capable middle class, an influential military and a potentially influential government and diplomacy[1]. However, India is considered the classic underachiever compared to other great powers while desiring to do great things it is nonetheless reluctant and appears inept in mobilizing the required confidence and action[2]. Furthermore, Guha has commented that India's pursuit of great power distracts the government from tackling the massive issues of illiteracy, poverty, and social and economic inequity[3]. Some Indian states have faired better than others[4]. Governance correspondingly suffers owing to coalition governments at the Centre and in the regions[5].

The apprehension about India's appropriate role overseas is furthermore tied to the country's complex situation at home. Also, the struggle against hunger in India cannot be achieved without creating a more devoted and just community and a state, which is committed to implementing the egalitarian goals of the country's continuing democratic form. Importantly, India's soft power remains ineffective for two immediate causes[6]. First, Indian diplomacy has ignored soft power as an important tool of statecraft and has only lately comprehended the relevance of CD[7]. Second, soft power cannot exist without some initial hard power achievements[8]. A nation will only be able to tell a more acceptable story if it has the material power to construct its soft power.

Most critics simply acknowledge soft power doesn't function in IR while presenting little substantial proof to support these claims[9]. Soft power has absolute limitations, and there are real challenges to its adequate use in global politics[10]. Nevertheless, these challenges are not so much thought of soft power's utility, but instead its political desirability, none of which question its validity or efficacy[11]. Critics' further state that soft power cannot substitute hard power and it helps only if the country has built up its conventional sources of economic and military power. For a developing country like India with multiple competing demands for scarce soft power resources its engagement has at times lacked policy coherence and efficacy. Nevertheless, due to India's status as a global power, a consolidated democracy and a country, that is free from colonial influence, its increasing role in the contemporary world affairs is likely to bolster its soft power in the coming years notwithstanding the limitations. As Nye himself has admitted, "Drinking coke or watching a Bollywood film does not automatically convey power for the U.S. or India[12]. Whether the possession of soft power resources produces favorable outcomes depends upon the context, which is often one of hard geopolitics[13]. Soft power is thus one arrow in a nation's security quiver and is not an all-purpose panacea[14]. Thus, India needs to articulate a clear grand strategy to project its soft power. Ultimately, my aim is to add to the debate on the usefulness of soft power and this empirical analysis in the book will further help shape the ongoing discussion.

The post-COVID world would certainly bring new challenges and opportunities for India. However, It's complicated to specifically foretell how the world would be molded with these circumstances in the long-drawn phase. India should figure out its strengths if it wants to resurrect its national image. The nation's potential of soft power if implemented certainly would enhance India's more exalted position, in making it well disposed and flourishing in the world. India needs to determine where its forces lie as it attempts to make the 21st century it's own. In the mounting multipolar global order, India definitely has the potential and holds immense opportunities to elevate its position further as the 'rising global soft power' that can further pave way for the country to become a 'soft power-superpower' of this century.

The influence of soft power varies according to each country. It is seen that while one country may like a certain cultural aspect, another country may not find that aspect interesting and influential. Soft power on whole is significant not only for a nation's position in the world but also it is necessary for identity and prosperity. India's growing economic and security profile in the contemporary world has found greater acceptance regionally and at the world stage India is seen as a non-threatening, benign power. According to Indian foreign policy analyst C Raja Mohan, India holds "strong cards in the arena of soft power" to further its foreign policy goals[15]. Furthermore, the use of hard power generally carries with it mass global public disapproval whereas soft power constitutes a country's principal asset. Presently, soft power in India has become an important instrument in PD, foreign policy and CSOs besides complementing official diplomacy efforts such as act east policy, the connect central Asia policy, developing strategic aid, implementing soft power matrix, trade partnerships in Africa etc. Additionally, increased cultural exchanges are more likely to increase public knowledge and appreciation of India in foreign countries. Also, It is argued that hard power is the underpinning from which soft power draws its efficacy, durability and outreach. Without hard power, soft power has little power, strength or viability. However despite some validity in the last statement, India tends to better deploy the portfolio of its soft power assets to facilitate long-term strategic ambitions and interests. Thus, despite large amount of literature, much remains to be comprehended about soft power and nation branding because attraction is a subjective understanding constructed by cultural industriousness.

Soft power is considered hard to quantify, therefore it is hard to measure its success[16]. Hard power, which is concentrated more on measurable resources, is known to be a straightforward counting game, and thus are the consequences of its applications[17]. On the contrary, soft power focuses on changing attitudes that is a hard task to which to assign a level or number[18]. Quantifying the successes of soft power can function, while the procedure becomes much more qualitative over quantitative activity[19]. Likewise, the strategic goals of soft power are more transparent and more directly translated in the active stages of performance[20]. Some scholars bound to the realist school of IR are resistant to assessing the possible efficacy of soft power because much of soft power is dependent on non-state actors considered unrelated by the principles of realism[21]. Yet, most critics merely acknowledge that soft power doesn't work in IR, though they present little substantial proof to back these claims[22]. Soft power has absolute constraints or limitations, and there are real challenges to its practical usage in international politics[23]. Nevertheless, these problems are not considered so much introspection of soft power's utility, but rather its political desirability, none of which challenge its validity or effectiveness[24]. In the domain of soft power, future researchers could indeed consider profusely researching the new ways that this study has demonstrated[25]. While researchers need to understand that soft power, innovative initiatives etc. are interdisciplinary entities of research, which include much more of this uncharted world to analyze or study[26].

The relevance, significance, and influence of soft power are impossible to overlook[27]. The fast evolution of the soft-power concept has made its central concept one of the most recognizable terms in the domain of IR[28]. Nye argues that soft power is a mechanism for success in global politics for those that know how to enhance it[29]. The increased usage of the concept of soft power in political discussion globally has been paralleled by significant intensification of research exercise on the subject[30]. The expansion of studies engaging the notion of soft power presently has become one of the most recognizable concepts in the domain of IR[31]. There have been few measures to provide an outline of soft power and systematize the fundamental accomplishments and unresolved issues in the domain[32]. Nye's work is considered the significant reference point within the content of scholarly literature on soft power as he not only coined the following concept but has also become the most prolific author on the topic[33]. Nye presents that soft power has a prolonged functional time frame compared to hard power and is better suitable for the accomplishment of general rather than specific objectives[34]. Also, Nye asserts that the control over soft power does not lie solely with a state's government, but is shared with civil society[35].

However, even though soft power concept has its origins elsewhere, scholars nonetheless admit the fact that Nye was the one who coined the concept of "soft power" and even connect their opinions against his[36]. While Nye's approach was first introduced in his book "Bound to Lead: The Changing Nature of American Power", his approach is best evolved in his books "Soft Power: The Means to Success in World Politics" and "The Future of Power"[37]. Nevertheless, majority of authors state that the notion of soft power requires modification, even though they conform to some prominent principles of Nye's understanding that might be deemed complicated[38]. There are likewise authors who would assert that soft power originated with Nye, further disputing that he only described ancient practices by expressing articulately in a way that suits the prevalent modern perspective on global politics that further captures contemporary advances in technology[39]. It is further observed that Nye's perspective of soft power has been considered by critical scholars to have a western centric edge[40]. Authors have therefore come to question the idea that the west alone or countries with democratic institutions can create or deliver soft power[41]. They have further exposed Nye for taking a supposed ubiquitous appeal of liberal-democratic values as paramount to soft power in general[42].

It is widely evident that India has tremendous soft power capability while the actuality remains that it has not been influential in developing enough of it due to several social and economic problems. Therefore, till these challenges are tackled appropriately, India will not be competent to project its soft power properly. The country's path towards $10 trillion economy by the mid 2030s will shape and be shaped by its foreign policy preferences in the decade ahead. India will indeed be a 'bridge nation' in the coming decade and will continue responding to its 20th century development challenges, even as millions of Indians embrace digital technologies to influence political developments and construct further pathways for social and economic mobility.

The COVID pandemic has uncovered the resource ineptitudes of governments, supply chain risks of businesses, and the inherent social and economic inequalities in civil societies, resulting in isolated countries, fragile economies and an inward-looking world. To address these daunting impediments and to create more peaceful, inclusive communities, more efficient and transparent rules ought to be set in a position with realistic and comprehensive government budgets. Furthermore, there are many gaps and challenges overlooked by the state in the area of development in a developing country such as India, where the civil societies need to permeate in modern India. Also, there is an unusual increase of conflict between the state and civil society as the needs and beliefs of the community are not being met. Unless there is no right equilibrium, co-operation and progress at the domestic and civil society level concerning the significant indicators of soft power like health, education, media etc. the country can not leverage its status at the global platform despite focusing to be one of the top economies globally.

GOI likewise needs to play a prominent role in augmenting governance through modern age diplomacy approaches to suit the modern era foreign policy of India. Among India's most important foreign policy priorities this decade will be steering the rapidly altering mental maps of the world. The free flow of ideas, innovations and technologies is a prerequisite for India's continuous advancement. The coming decade will increasingly see the diaspora place new directions on India's foreign policy. India is a "status quo power" but it must build an institution that will lead to long-term planning. The coming decade will further test India's capability to exert its influence as a great power does. Undoubtedly, the most crucial function this decade will be India's quest for a 'consensus' and an overarching framework to organize the efforts of its state and society and the global community.

In the contemporary global order that is looking for institutional structures leveled in the rule of law, India will have to further contribute to a much-required renewal of multilateralism. The country has been greatly influential in boosting the demands of the global south in various multilateral organizations, occasionally working in coalitions, occasionally independently. If India indulges in a policy of do not provoke and nor get provoked, exploit its rising soft power prospects completely and focus on constructing up a more vibrant and robust economy, then this could well be an accentuation point in India's rise as a global power. India understands that the global order is in a state of instability with the rise of a more assertive China and Russia, the shifts unfolding in Europe even as the U.S is in a situation of reorienting itself on nationalistic lines. There has been debate over the last few years about India as an international soft power. Nevertheless, in the age of greater globalization and measures by others to dominate IR, India requires refining its current approach where it carves out its rightful position in the world.

Former Indian diplomat Syed Akbaruddin asserted, "Soft power requires loud platforms and hard money". So, to enhance its soft power, GOI should consider investing more and formulate unique and distinct strategies to enrich the country's soft power. Today, India presently confronts tension on numerous facades such as soft power, economic and military. The hindrances to soft power are compounded by fortes like the economic deceleration that could impact India's power to influence others, and military coercion generated by discord in South Asia. Also, "Quiet diplomacy" that is established in areas such as culture, civilization and spiritualism, or merely attaining a fondness for India is consequently important in the advancement of soft power. Nevertheless, more needs to be done on the domestic front to use it. A strong civil society therefore reinforces citizens' respect for the state and facilitates their positive commitment to it. Also, a democratic state cannot be long lasting unless it is fair and effective, with the consideration and backing of its citizens. The promises of democracy can solely be acknowledged through collaborative efforts in civil society.

Soft power is not promoted to its true potential either due to lack of proper promoting strategies or mostly it is confined to a particular stream alone by the GOI rather than promoting whole soft powers like art, music, medicine, architecture, cuisines, culture etc. and most of the soft power instruments were self promoting such as Yoga. Nevertheless, GOI should analyze this pattern and ensure proper strategies are formalized for each of the above-mentioned attributes and promotions should be made. India still seems to be in a state where it recognizes its soft power capacities but does not yet know how best to deploy them. If India aspires to be a global power, it needs to build a strong economic foundation and further be more proactive and vocal in the external arena besides using interest-based diplomacy. India has been very successful in using its soft power potential due to its culture, history and cuisine, which are popular all over the world. However, Indian image globally is centered on more traditional aspects, and as a consequence modern India with its vibrant science, innovations and hi-tech sector is not widely known and these aspects should be better stressed globally.

Tharoor in the book "The great Indian novel" remarked that India is not, as people keep calling it an underdeveloped country, but rather in the context of its history and cultural heritage, a highly developed one in an advanced state of decay. The Nehruvian vision of a peaceful and democratic world should thus remain an inspiration for India, with the promotion of a peaceful regional order serving as a stepping-stone to this vision. Nehru and other leaders strived for inspiration from ancient and medieval India.

Also, leaders from Nehru to Modi have further promised to restore India to its eminence but there should be additional institutional building in foreign policy. Indian policy-making depends on the vision and will of its leader. So, India should correspondingly expand its educational and professional exchange programs with IOs and universities, and at the same time invite eminent fellows of civil society of other countries to foster a better insight into Indian culture, interests and values, so that they can portray the country in a good light. Augmenting funding for cultural activities in Indian embassies and consulates can likewise additionally enhance India's PD. Though gradually, India is more presumably to maintain its course of life and its civilization of diversity, tolerance and spirituality against the onslaught of the global culture.

In the near future, the world will be more multi-conceptual: power will be diffused among institutions, non-state actors, civil society and cities and defying hierarchical state control. The survival or reform of the international liberal order will depend entirely on new stakeholders and advocates and India will be prominent among them. The advancement of India is the topic of significant debate both among Indians and the global community. American scholar, Stephen Cohen commented that India, whether a realist or an idealist, almost every member of the Indian strategic community acknowledges that India's innate superiority as a power is itself a priceless diplomatic asset[43]. Former Indian diplomat Shiv Shankar Menon in the book "Choices: Inside the making of India's foreign policy" further mentioned how PM Indira Gandhi once stated, "India will be a different power and will continue to tread its own path in the world". In this context, a self-assured and progressive India will be good for its citizens and the hope is that the new multilateralism setting will contribute to India's growth, development and national confidence.

Furthermore, Mahatma Gandhi's quote, "True power speaks softly, it has no reason to shout", and Lao Tse quote, "Water is the softest thing, yet it can penetrate mountains and the earth", illustrates the postulate of softness subduing hardness. It is thus important for India to join the dots of its soft power strengths to raise its soft power profile. Aparna Pande in the book "Making India Great: The promise of a reluctant global power" mentions that "Ancient India was isolationist, which modern India cannot afford to be. Ancient India was otherworldly, but modern India needs to succeed and exercise power in this world. Only that would make India great in the eyes of the world". So, in this view despite emphasizing on India's hard power the role of its soft power will indeed be of prominent importance in the coming years. Thus, as discussed in the book, GOI continues to exert its soft power, the role of civil society and the non-state actors will become important as it will continue to enhance its influence in the coming years.

Notes

1. Karnad. (2015) *Why India Is Not A Great Power (yet)*. London: Oxford university press.
2. *Ibid.*
3. *Ibid.*
4. *Ibid.*
5. *Ibid.*
6. Blarel, N (2012) India: the next superpower?: India's soft power: from potential to reality? *IDEAS Reports: special reports*, LSE IDEAS, London School of Economics and Political Science, London, UK.
7. *Ibid.*
8. *Ibid.*
9. Seymour, M. (2020). The problem with soft power, Foreign policy research Institute. *Transnational social review*, 6 (1/2): 141–159
10. *Ibid.*
11. *Ibid.*
12. Tharoor,S (2007) *The land of the better story: India and soft power*. Global Asia, 2(1), April: 70–76.
13. *Ibid.*
14. *Ibid.*
15. Ramachandran, S.(2015) *India's soft power potential*. Available at: https://thediplomat.com/2015/05/indias-soft-power-potential/ (Accessed: 12 May 2022).
16. Seymour, M. (2020). The problem with soft power, Foreign policy research Institute. *Transnational social review*, 6 (1/2): 141–159
17. *Ibid.*
18. *Ibid.*
19. *Ibid.*
20. *Ibid.*
21. *Ibid.*
22. *Ibid.*
23. *Ibid.*
24. *Ibid.*
25. *Ibid.*
26. *Ibid.*
27. Thomson (2020) *Soft Power: Why it Matters to Governments, People, and Brands*. Available at: https://brandfinance.com/insights/soft-power-why-it-matters (Accessed: 15 May 2022).

28. *Ibid.*
29. *Ibid.*
30. Bakalov, I. (2019), Whither soft power? Divisions, milestones, and prospects of a research Programme in the making, *Journal Of Political Power*, 12(1), 129-151. DOI: 10.1080/2158379X.2019.1573613
31. *Ibid.*
32. *Ibid.*
33. *Ibid.*
34. *Ibid.*
35. *Ibid.*
36. *Ibid.*
37. *Ibid.*
38. *Ibid.*
39. *Ibid.*
40. *Ibid.*
41. *Ibid.*
42. *Ibid.*
43. Ani (2022) *Jaishankar to launch 'Connecting through Culture', an anthology on India's soft power.* Available at: https://theprint.in/india/jaishankar-to-launch-connecting-through-culture-an-Anthology-on-India's-soft-power/1034767/ (Accessed: 16 May 2022)

Bibliography

Institutions Visited

1. The Nehru Memorial Library Archives, New Delhi (India).
2. The National Archives of India, New Delhi (India).
3. Moscow State Institute of International Relations library, (Russia).
4. Stellenbosch University library, (South Africa).
5. Connemara Public Library, Chennai (India).

Journal Articles

1. Adesina. (2017) Foreign policy in an era of digital diplomacy. *Cogent Social Sciences*. 3:1, DOI: 10.1080/23311886.2017.1297175
2. Bajpai, S. (2021), Pulse of Soft Power in India's Foreign Policy: Exploring the derivative potential of COVID-19 diplomacy, *Academia Letters*, Article 1031. DOI: 10.20935/AL1031.
3. Bajpai. K, Chong. B. (2019) India's Foreign Policy Capacity, *Policy Design and Practice*, 2:2, 137-162.
4. Bilgin, P., & Eli°, B. (2008). Hard Power, Soft Power: Toward a More Realistic Power Analysis. *Insight Turkey, 10*, 5
5. Blarel, Paliwal (2019) Opening the black box – The making of India's foreign policy, *India Review*, 18:5, 457 470, DOI: 10.1080/14736489.2019.1703359.
6. Boesche (2003) Kautilya's Arthasastra on War and Diplomacy in Ancient India, The Journal of Military History, Volume 67, Number 1, pp. 9-37, *Society for Military History*, DOI: 10.1353/jmh.2003.0006.
7. Bolewski, W., Sandu, D. (2021). Emotional Intelligence in Foreign Policy Processes. *Academia Letters*, Article 1245. DOI: 10.20935/AL1245.
8. Car, Viduka, Kosstanisic. (2016) The limits of soft power public diplomacy, *Teorija in Praksha,* let. 53, 5/2016
9. Ciorciari, J. D. (2011) India's Approach to Great-Power Status. *The Fletcher Forum of World Affairs*, *35*(1), 61–89.
10. Dellios, R (2003) China and India: New mandalas of power in 21st century geopolitics. in RN Gnosh, MA Siddique & R Gabbay (eds), *Essays on development issues: India and the Indian Ocean region.* Atlantic, New Delhi, pp. 93-113.

11. Erickson, A. S., & Strange, A. M. (2015). China's blue soft power: Antipiracy, Engagement, and Image Enhancement. *Naval War College Review*, *68*(1), 71–92.
12. Hall. I (2012), "India's New Public Diplomacy", *Asian Survey*, pp. 1089-1110, Vol. 52, No. 6
13. Happymon, J., & Hall, I. (2016) Review of The Engagement of India: Strategies and Responses. *European Review of International Studies*, *3*(1), 142–144.
14. Harvey. (2015) The price of free speech in India today, Socialist Lawyer, No. 71 *Pluto Journals*, pp. 32-33.
15. Hunter, A. (2009). Soft Power: China on the Global Stage. *The Chinese Journal of International Politics*, *2*(3), 373–398.
16. 16. Hymans. J. E. C (2009) India's Soft Power and Vulnerability, *India Review* 8(3): 234-265, DOI: 10.1080/14736480903116784.
17. Kapur, D (2012). Diaspora Development and Democracy: The Domestic Impact of International Migration from India. 344p. Perspectives on Politics. *Princeton University Press*. DOI: 10. 216-217.10.1017/S1537592711004774.
18. Karnad, B. (2015). India's strategic diffidence: What does India think? *European Council on Foreign Relations*, (pp. 85–89)
19. Kivimäki, T. (2014). Soft Power and Global Governance with Chinese Characteristics. *The Chinese Journal of International Politics*, *7*(4), 421–447.
20. Krishna, S. M. (2009) India's Foreign Policy Priorities. *India Quarterly*, *65*(4), 345–349.
21. Kunwar, R. (2021). Politics and Diplomacy in COVID Pandemic. *Academia Letters,* Article 1719. DOI: 10.20935/AL1719.
22. Lahiri,S. (2017) Soft power – A major tool in Modi's foreign policy kit. *Journal of South Asian Studies, 5*, 39-47.
23. Leira (2019) The Emergence of Foreign Policy, *Norwegian Institute of International Affairs (NUPI),* International Studies Quarterly (2019) 63, 187–198.
24. Li, M. (2020) Chinese Television and Soft Power Communication in Australia. *Anthem Press*. https://doi.org/10.2307/j.ctvsn3ntq.
25. Lissner, R., & Rapp-Hooper, M. (2020). *An Open World: How America Can Win the Contest for Twenty-First-Century Order*. *Yale university press*. Doi: 10.2307/j.ctv15pjxfp.
26. Mahapatra, C. (2018). India: The New Power in the Emerging Global Order. *Indian Foreign Affairs Journal*, *13*(2), 101–106.
27. Mahapatra, D. (2016) From a latent to a 'strong' soft power? The evolution of India's cultural diplomacy, *Palgrave Commun* 2, 16091(2016). DOI: 10.1057/palcomms.2016.91.
28. Mansingh. S (2010), Assessing Reorientation of India's Foreign Policy in a Globalized World, *International Studies, 47, 2–4 (2010): 143–161*
29. Mazumdar. A (2020), India's Public Diplomacy in the Twenty-First Century: Components, Objectives and Challenges, *ICWA*, India Quarterly 76(1) 24–39, 2020.

30. Murti, Zaharna. (2014) Indias Digital Diaspora Diplomacy: Operationalizing Collaborative Public Diplomacy Strategies for Social Media, *Exchange: The Journal of Public Diplomacy,* Vol. 5 [2014], Iss. 1, Art. 3.

31. Mutatkar, R. (2011) State, Civil Society and Justice: The Case of India. Global Civil Society. *Palgrave Macmillan*, DOI: 10.1057/9780230303805_18.

32. Racine, J.L (2008). Post-Post-Colonial India: From Regional Power to Global Player. *Politique Étrangère*, *73*, 65–78.

33. Shekhawat, V. S. (2010). Terror topography and India's soft underbelly. *The Indian Journal of Political Science*, *71*(4), 1185–1200.

34. Suri. N (2011), Public Diplomacy in India's Foreign Policy, *Strategic Analysis*, 35:2, 297-303, DOI: 10.1080/09700161.2011.542927

35. Tripathi, A. (2011). Prospects of India becoming a Global Power. *Indian Foreign Affairs Journal*, *6*(1), 58–69.

36. Thussu, D. K (2016) The soft power of popular cinema – the case of India, *Journal of Political Power*, 9:3, 415-429, DOI: 10.1080/2158379X.2016.1232288.

37. Varshney. A (2001) Ethnic Conflict and Civil Society: India and Beyond, World Politics, *Cambridge University Press*, Vol. 53, No. 3, pp. 362-398.

38. Verma (2018) The Role of the private sector in India's economic diplomacy: Opportunities and Challenges, *Zenith International Journal of Multidisciplinary Research,* Vol.8 (8), pp. 150-165

39. Wang, Y. (2008). Public Diplomacy and the Rise of Chinese Soft Power. *The Annals of the American Academy of Political and Social Science*, *616*, 257–273

Books, Reports and Thesis

Books

40. Abbas, Alam, Kumar. (2010) *Indian Government and Politics*. India: Pearson.

41. Aiyar. (2007) *Globalization in Indian civil society responses*. Pune: National Centre for Advocacy studies

42. Atri, N (2019) *Brainwashed Republic: India's Controlled Systemic Deracination*. New Delhi: Abhishek Publications.

43. Bajpai, Pant. (2013) *India's Foreign Policy: A Reader*. London: Oxford University Press

44. Bandyopadhyay, S. (2014) *From Plassey To Partition And After*. Hyderabad: Orient Blackswan.

45. Bandyopadhyaya. (1970) *Making of India's foreign policy*. Bombay: Allied publications.

46. Baru, S (2021) *Beyond COVID Shadow: Mapping India's Economic Resurgence* New Delhi: Rupa.

47. Baru. S (2021) *India's Power elite: Caste, class and Cultural Revolution*. New Delhi: Penguin Books India.

48. Bhagwati, J. (2019) *The Promise of India: How Prime Ministers Nehru to Modi Shaped the Nation (1947–2019)*. New York: Penguin Viking.

49. Berkes. R (1958) *Diplomacy of India: Indian foreign policy in the United Nations.* California: Stanford university press
50. Chandra, Mukherjee, Mukherjee (2008) *India Since Independence*. New Delhi: Penguin Random House India.
51. Chandhoke, Priyadarshi (2009) *Contemporary India: Economy, Society, Politics*, New Delhi: Pearson.
52. Chikermane, G (2021) *India 2030: Rise of a Rajasic Nation: A deep dive into India's financial and economic policies*. New Delhi: Penguin eBury Press.
53. Cooper, Heine, Thakur (2013) *The Oxford book of Modern Diplomacy*. London: Oxford university press.
54. Dogra. R (2020) *India's World - (HB): How prime ministers shaped foreign policy*, New Delhi: Rupa Publications India.
55. Damodaran. (1987) *Heritage of Indian foreign policy circa: 1966: Seminar"- Seminar on Indian foreign policy under Indira Gandhi*. New Delhi: NMML
56. Danino, M. (2011) *Indian Culture and India's Future*. New Delhi: D.K. Print World Ltd.
57. Das, G. (2012) *The Difficulty of Being Good: On the Subtle Art of Dharma.* New Delhi: Penguin India.
58. Das, G (2012) *The elephant paradigm- India wrestles with change*. New Delhi: Penguin.
59. Das, G (2012) *India Grows at Night - A Liberal Case for a Strong State*. New Delhi: Penguin India.
60. Daulet, S.Z (2018) *Power and Diplomacy: India's Foreign Policies During the Cold War*. London: Oxford University Press.
61. Debroy, Tellis, Trevor. (2014) *Getting India Back on Track: An Action Agenda for Reform.* New Delhi: Vintage.
62. Drèze, Chomsky. (2020). *Democracy and Power: The Delhi Lectures*, Indiana: Saint Philip Street Press
63. Dreze, Sen. (2013) *An Uncertain Glory: India and its Contradictions*. London: Penguin.
64. Dubey. M. (2017) *India's Foreign Policy: Coping With The Changing World*. Hyderabad: The Orient Blackswan.
65. Dutt, V.P (2007) *India's foreign policy: Since independence*. New Delhi: National Book Trust.
66. Dogra, R (2020) *India's World - (HB): How prime ministers shaped foreign policy*, New Delhi: Rupa.
67. Ganguly, S. (2011) *India's Foreign Policy: Retrospect and Prospect*. London: Oxford university press.
68. Gautier, F. G (2020) *An Entirely New History of INDIA: Translated from French 'Nouvelle Histoire de l'Inde'*. Gurugram: Garuda Prakasham.
69. Gupta. (2020) *India's foreign policy: Surviving in a turbulent world*. California: SAGE.
70. Guha, R (2012) *Makers of Modern India*. New Delhi: Penguin India.

71. Hall, H. (2019) *Modi and the Reinvention of Indian Foreign Policy*. Bristol: Policy press.
72. Huntington, S. (2016) *The Clash of Civilization and the Remaking of World Order*. New York: Random House.
73. Jha, S. (2010) *India and China: the battle between soft and hard power*. New Delhi: Penguin.
74. Jayaram. (2005) On civil society: issues and perspectives. California: SAGE.
75. Kamath, P.M. (2014) *India as an emerging major power: foreign policy thrust areas*. New Delhi: ICWA.
76. Kant, A (2018) *The Path Ahead: Transformative Ideas for India*. New Delhi: Rupa Publications.
77. Karnad, B (2018) *Staggering Forward: Narendra Modi and India's Global Ambition*. New York: Penguin Viking.
78. Khanna, P (2019) *The Future Is Asian: Commerce, Conflict, and Culture in the 21st Century*. New York: Simon & Schuster.
79. Kishan, Thussu. (2016) *Communicating India's Soft Power: Buddha To Bollywood* California: SAGE.
80. Khilnani, S. (2001) *Civil society: history and possibilities*. London: Cambridge University Press.
81. Khilnani, N.M (1981) *Panorama of Indian diplomacy: From Mauryan epoch to post- Nehru era*. New Delhi: S. Chand and Company
82. Kugiel, P (2016) *India's Soft Power: A New Foreign Policy Strategy*. New Delhi: KW Publishers.
83. Kumar. (1998) *Rethinking civil society.* Chennai: Madras Institute of development studies.
84. Kumar, S (2017) *Indian Society*. New Delhi: Pearson India.
85. Li, M 2020, *Chinese television and soft power communication in Australia*. London: Anthem Press
86. Jalan, B (2018) *India ahead: 2025 and beyond*. New Delhi: Rupa.
87. Madhusudan, Mantri (2020) *A New Idea of India: Individual Rights in a Civilizational State*, New Delhi: Westland.
88. Mohan, R (2015) *Modi's World: Expanding India's Sphere of Influence*. New Delhi: HarperCollins India
89. Malhotra, R (2013) *Being Different: An Indian Challenge To Western Universalism.* New York: HarperCollins.
90. Mander, H (2012) *Ash in the belly*, New Delhi: Penguin.
100. Mander, Bhattacharya, Mishra, Singla, Siddiqi. (2019) *Unequal Life Chances: Equity and the Demographic Transition in India*. California: SAGE.
101. Menon, S. (2021) *India and Asian Geopolitics: The Past, Present*, Washington D.C: Brookings Institution.
102. Menon, S. (2016) *Choices: Inside the Making of Indian Foreign Policy.* New Delhi: Penguin Random House India.
103. Menon, S (2021) *India and Asian Geopolitics: The Past, Present.* Washington. D.C: Brookings Institution.

104. Muller, Max. (2002) *India: What can it teach us?* New Delhi: Rupa.

105. Nye, J. (2011) *The Future of Power*, New York: Perseus.

106. Mukherjee, A. (2019) *The Absent Dialogue*. London: Oxford University Press.

107. Panagariya. (2020) *India Unlimited: Reclaiming the Lost Glory*. New Delhi: Harper India.

108. Pande, A. (2020) *Making India Great: The Promise of a Reluctant Global Power*. New York: HarperCollins.

111. Pant, HV. (2019) *Indian Foreign Policy: The Modi Era*. New Delhi: Har-Anand Publications.

112. Pattnaik, S. (1982) *India's foreign policy: Basic issues and political attitudes*. London: Oxford university press.

113. Raghavan. (2007) *Civil society and governance in modern India*. Chennai: East west books.

114. Rajshekar, M. (2021) *Despite the State: Why India Lets Its People Down and How They Cope*. New Delhi: Context.

115. Rathod. P. B. (2009) *Foreign policy of India*. New Delhi: Commonwealth publication.

116. Ray, DD. (2015) *The Making of Indian Diplomacy: A Critique of Eurocentrism* London: Oxford university press.

117. Sandre. A (2015) *Digital Diplomacy: Conversations on Innovation in Foreign Policy*, Lanham: Rowman & Littlefield.

118. Sanyal, S. (2013) *Land of the Seven Rivers: A Brief History of India's Geography*. New Delhi: Penguin India.

119. Sanyal, S. (2015) *The Indian Rennaissance: India's Rise after a Thousand Years of Decline*. London: Penguin

120. Sanyal, S. (2016) *The Ocean of Churn: How the Indian Ocean Shaped Human History*. New Delhi: Penguin Random House India.

121. Sanyal, Rajendran (2015) *The Incredible History of India's Geography*. New York: Penguin Books Limited

122. Saran, S. (2017) *How India sees the world: From Kautilya to Modi: Kautilya to the 21st Century*. New Delhi: Juggernaut.

123. Shah (2018) *Democracy, civil society and governance*. California: SAGE.

124. Shanks. (1995) *Civil society, civil religion*. London: Oxford: Blackwell.

125. Sharma. R (2012) *Breakout Nations: In pursuit of the Next Economic Miracles*. London: Penguin U.K.

126. Sharma. R (2019) *Democracy on the Road: A 25-Year Journey through India*. London: Penguin U.K.

127. Sharma, R. (2016) *The Rise and Fall of Nations: Ten Rules of Change in the Post-Crisis World*. London: Penguin U.K.

128. Singh (2018) *Governance: Issues and Challenges*. New Delhi: Pearson

129. Singh. I (1946), India's foreign policy, Bombay: Hind Kitab

130. Snow, Taylor. (2009) *Routledge Handbook of Public Diplomacy*, London: Routledge

131. Sreenivasan (2008) *Applied Diplomacy: Through the Prism of Mythology*. New Delhi: Wisdom Tree.

132. Thapar, R (2003) *The Penguin History of Early India: From the Origins to AD 1300*. New Delhi: Penguin India.

133. Tharoor, S (2020) *The Battle Of Belonging: On Nationalism, Patriotism, And What It Means To Be Indian*. New Delhi: Aleph Book Company.

134. Tharoor, S (2016) *An Era of Darkness: The British Empire in India*. New Delhi: Aleph

135. Tharoor. S (2014). *The Great Indian Novel*. New York: Penguin.

136. Tharoor, S. (2016) *The Idea of India*. New Delhi: Random House India.

137. Tharoor, Saran. (2020) *The New World Disorder and the Indian Imperative*. New Delhi: Aleph Book Company.

138. Tharoor. S (2015) *India Shastra: Reflections on the Nation in our Time*. New Delhi: Aleph Book Company.

139. Tharoor. S (2012) *India: From Midnight to the Millennium*. New Delhi: Penguin India.

140. Thussu, D. (2016) *Communicating India's Soft Power: Buddha To Bollywood*. New Delhi: SAGE Vistaar.

141. Winder, R (2020) *Soft Power: The New Great Game for Global Dominance*. Boston: Little & Brown.

Reports

142. Bornstein, Johnson, Mohtadi, Park, Weiss (2015), "*Civil Societies: Empowering constituencies in India & Pakistan*", Spring Capstone report, viewed June 14 2020, Columbia School of International affairs and public relations

143. Hill, Beadle (2014), *The Art of Attraction Soft Power and the UK's Role in the World*, The British Academy, viewed 3 March 2021, The British Academy, U.K.

144. Kishwar, S (2018), "*The Rising Role of Buddhism in India's Soft Power Strategy*", Issue no. 228, ORF issue brief, viewed August 3 2021, ORF.

145. Kode, Jacob, Firmin (2017), "*India: Democracy threatened by growing attacks on civil society*", CIVICUS, viewed April 13 2020, CIVICUS.

146. Lettinga, Troost. (2015), *Shifting Power and Human Rights Diplomacy*, Amnesty International Netherlands report, viewed 7 August 2020, Amnesty database.

147. Levaillant, M (2017), *"Diplomacy as Diaspora Management: The Case of India and the Gulf States"*, Asie.Visions, No.95, viewed 14 August 2020, Ifri.

148. MacDonald (2018), "*Power of attraction: Young people's views on the soft power of the G20 group of nations*", British Council, Viewed 12 May 2020, British Council U.K.

149. Manor, I (2018), *"The Digitalization of Diplomacy: Toward Clarification of a Fractured Terminology"*, DigDiploROx Working Paper No 2, viewed 8 October *2020,* University of Oxford.

150. Mazumdar, Nag (2021), *"Imagining India in the post-COVID world: An analysis of possible pathways*", Vol 8, Issue 6, Viewed 4 January, 2022, India @73, The Diplomatist.

151. MT, Sahgal. (2019), *"India's Soft Power: Challenges and Opportunities",* Rajiv Gandhi Institute for Contemporary Studies, viewed 19 July 2020, RGICS.

152. Pant, Taneja (2019), "*Looking Back and Looking Ahead: Indian Foreign Policy in Transition Under Modi*", ORF Special Report No. 93, viewed June 11 2020, ORF.

153. P. Samaj (200), *Overview of civil society organizations*, Civil society briefs, viewed 3 February 2021, Asian Development Bank.

154. Wang (2014), *"Cooperation with India: An Option or A Must?, Hamdania, Rising soft powers, India"*, CPD, viewed July 13 2020, USC Center on Public Diplomacy.

155. Youngs, R. (2018), "*The Ascent of conservative civil society in India"*, Carnegie Endowment for International Peace, viewed 9 November 2020, Carnegie Endowment.

Thesis

156. Fergus, S.A (2011), *U.S foreign policy: Domestic pluralism and the search for a grand strategy for China*, Doctoral thesis, Durham University, England, viewed 21 July 2020, <http://etheses.dur.ac.uk/3345/1/Fergus_-_PhD_Thesis_(2011).pdf?DDD35+>.

157. Liang (2017), *The effectiveness of cultural diplomacy in state trust building between China and the U.K*, PhD thesis, Lancaster University, U.K, viewed 13 June 2020, < https://eprints.lancs.ac.uk/id/eprint/124992/1/2018liangPhD.pdf>

158. Patkar, N .G (2017), *India's Mediated Public Diplomacy on Social Media: Building Agendas and National Reputation in South Asia*, PhD thesis, Scripps College of Communication of Ohio University, U.S, viewed 19 June 2020, <https://etd.ohiolink.edu/apexprod/rws_etd/send_file/send?accession=ohiou1510166260357 57&disposition=inline>

159. Patalakh, A (2017), *Soft power revisited: What attraction is in International relations*, Doctoral thesis, University of Milan, Italy, viewed 9 September 2021, <https://www.academia.edu/38760311/Soft_Power_Revisited_ What_Attraction_Is_in_International_Relations>

160. Pimpale, A (2017), *India and the Responsibility to Protect Norm: A Constructivist Analysis*, Masters Thesis, Leiden University, Netherlands, viewed 13 November 2019, < https://studenttheses.universiteitleiden.nl/access/item%3A2628807/view>.

161. Prasad, R (2019), *Could the United Nations Security Council be made more representative to include India? Case study: India's Leaders' historical experiences and future impacts,* Masters thesis, Leiden University, Netherlands, viewed 2 December, 2021, <https://studenttheses.universiteitleiden.nl/access/item%3A2629268/view>

162. Roy, N (2011), *A study of deviant state behavior: Indian foreign policy- 1947 to 1962*, PhD thesis, Carleton University, Canada, viewed 14 June 2020, https:/

/curve.carleton.ca/system/files/etd/a4afed25-b5d9-4da6-8540-ed82e64dcadd/etd_pdf/9eaf821cfd60f9db823c9864b5a02470/roy-astudyofdeviantstatebehaviorindianforeign.pdf.

Online Articles

163. Adeel. M (2017), "Digital Diplomacy and its role in Statecraft", https://stratagem.pk/geostrategy/digital-diplomacy-role-statecraft/ (Accessed: 18 August 2020)
164. Adnan, I. (2011) *In an Era of Soft Power, a Way Forward for Women*. Available at: https://www.huffpost.com/entry/in-an-era-of-soft-power-a_b_489692 (Accessed: 17 October 2020).
165. Amir, F. (2014) *Unmasking China's Assertive Behaviour in the Maritime Sphere*. Available at: https://www.e-ir.info/2014/09/29/unmasking-chinas-Assertive-behavior-in-the-maritime-sphere/ (Accessed: 4 October 2021).
166. Bagchi, P.(2020) *India's soft power in the age of hard Hindutva*. Available at: https://www.business-standard.com/article/opinion/india-s-soft-power-in-the-age-of-hard-hindutva-120030301802_1.html (Accessed: 5 October 2020)
167. Baru, S. (2021) *What's going wrong with India's Act East policy?*. Available at:https://indianexpress.com/article/opinion/columns/india-singapore-relationship-southeast-asia-policy-7330227/ (Accessed: 29 January 2022).
168. Betigeri, A. (2021) *India's beauty and the beast*. Available at https://www.lowyinstitute.org/the-interpreter/india-s-beauty-and-beast (Accessed: 29 January 2022)
169. Bhatia, R. (2011) *Public diplomacy — the tasks ahead*. Available at: https://www.thehindu.com/opinion/lead/Public-diplomacy-mdash-the-tasks-ahead/article15514526.ece (Accessed: 9 October 2020).
170. Bhattacharya, G. (2021) *India must use soft power effectively*. Available at: https://www.thestatesman.com/opinion/india-must-use-soft-power-effectively-1503024189.html (Accessed: 29 January 2022).
171. Bhasin, M. (2010) *India's Approach to Public Diplomacy in the Information Age*. Available at: https://foreignpolicyblogs.com/2010/12/10/indias-approach-to-public-diplomacy-in-the-information-age/ (Accessed: 22 April 2022).
172. Biswas. B, Goel. A. (2020) *Narendra Modi's soft-power diplomatic efforts abroad are being undone by hardline politics at home*", Available at: https://scroll.in/article/961333/narendra-modis-soft-power-diplomatic-efforts-abroad-are-being-undone-by-hardline-politics-at-home (Accessed: 12 November 2021)
173. Biswas, K. (2021) *The subtle art of soft power: How nations use culture to engage in a "storytelling competition.*

    Available at: https://www.newstatesman.com/culture/2021/07/Robert-winder-soft-power-great-game-review (Accessed: 21 August 2021)
174. Biswas. B, Goel. A. (2020) *India in the Security Council: Time to Step Up*. Available at:https://thediplomat.com/2020/12/india-in-the-security-council-time-to-step-up/ (Accessed: 14 January 2021)
175. Bhan, A. (2021) *India's global profile has taken wings. Available at:* https://www.sundayguardianlive.com/legally-speaking/indias-global-profile-taken-wings (Accessed: 17 September 2021)

176. Chang. E, Kim. N. (2016). *The Myth of Soft Power in Asia*. Available at: https://www.e-ir.info/2016/05/24/the-myth-of-soft-power-in-asia/ (Accessed: 3 March 2020)

177. Carminati. (2019) *China's Belt and Road Initiative: Debt Trap or Soft Power Catalyst*? Available at: https://www.e-ir.info/2019/09/01/chinas-belt-and-road-initiative-debt-trap-or-soft-power-catalyst/ (Accessed: 24 November 2021)

178. Chaudhury, D. R. (2016) *India on top 10 ranking of global digital diplomacy: Diplomacy Live*. Available at: https://economictimes.indiatimes.com/news/politics-and-nation/india-on-top-10-ranking-of-global-digital-diplomacy-diplomacy-live/articleshow/51715372.cms (Accessed: 24 December 2020).

179. Chaudhury, D. R. (2020) *India launches soft-power initiative to unite global citizens fighting Covid menace*. Available at: https://economictimes.indiatimes.com/news/politics-and-nation/india-launches-soft-power-initiative-to-unite-global-citizens-fighting-covid-menace/articleshow/74916444.cms (Accessed: 6 October 2020).

180. Chaudhury, D.R (2020) *Unlike China, India's soft power built through trust, credibility and democracy*. Available at: https://economictimes.indiatimes.com/news/politics-and-nation/unlike-china-indias-soft-power-built-through-trust-credibility-and-democracy/articleshow/79295115.cms, (Accessed: 18 February 2021).

181. Chen, X. (2018) *China in the Post-Hegemonic Middle East: A Wary Dragon?* Available at: https://www.e-ir.info/2018/11/22/china-in-the-post-hegemonic-middle-east-a-wary-dragon/ (Accessed: 17 January 2022).

182. Dar. Z.A, Raja. R. (2020) *Asian Security amid China's Dominance*. Available at: https://www.e-ir.info/2020/08/09/asian-security-amid-chinas-dominance/ (Accessed: 23 January 2022).

183. Dev, N. (2021) "India's Diwali As A Tool Of Soft Power In US – Op Ed", https://www.eurasiareview.com/09112021-indias-diwali-as-a-tool-of-soft-power-in-us-oped/ (Accessed: 18 February 2022).

184. Dubber, J. (2015) *How soft power can help meet international challenges*. Available at: https://www.britishcouncil.org/research-policy-insight/insight-articles/how-soft-power-can-help-meet-international-challenges (Accessed: 23 February 2021).

185. Elhusseini, F. (2016) *Soft Power in the Middle East: The Invisible Skirmish* Available at: https://www.e-ir.info/2016/08/08/soft-power-in-the-middle-east-the-invisible-skirmish/ (Accessed: 14 September 2020).

186. ET. (2015) *6 things Modi government is doing to make India a tourist hub*. Available at: https://economictimes.indiatimes.com/news/politics-and-nation/6-things-modi-government-is-doing-to-make-india-a-tourist-hub/articleshow/48186959.cms (Accessed: 10 October 2019)

187. Feng, C. (2021) *China in 'culture export' push as it seeks to expand soft power overseas with global media platforms*". Available at: https://www.scmp.com/tech/tech-trends/article/3154198/china-culture-export-push-it-seeks-expand-soft-power-overseas (Accessed: 17 January 2022).

188. Fensom. (2021) *2022 New Year's Resolutions for Asia's Biggest Economies*. Available at: https://thediplomat.com/2022/01/2022-new-years-resolutions-for-asias-biggest-economies/ (Accessed: 18 February 2022)

189. Fernandes, B. (2021) *The many benefits of a strong GI ecosystem*. Available at:https://indianexpress.com/article/opinion/columns/geographical-indications-ecosystem-e-commerce-climate-change-7544733/ (Accessed: 2 February 2022)

190. Ford, C. (2016) *When Soft Power Turns Hard: Miss World, Coercion and China's Cultural Diplomacy.* Available at: https://www.e-ir.info/2016/03/03/when-soft-power-turns-hard-miss-world-coercion-and-chinas-cultural-diplomacy/ (Accessed: 21 November 2021)

191. Game. (2021) *Broken Threads: Reshaping Multilateralism with COVID-19 under Way*. Available at: https://www.e-ir.info/2021/05/10/broken-threads-reshaping-multilateralism-with-covid-19-under-way/ (Accessed: 23 December 2021).

192. Ganguly, S. (2021) *Modi Spent India's Soft Power—and Got Little in Return*. Available at: https://foreignpolicy.com/2021/02/14/modi-india-power-farmer-protest-human-rights/ (Accessed: 18 December 2021).

193. Gontcharava, A. (2011) *China: 21st Century "Superpower"?* Available at: https://www.e-ir.info/2011/07/07/china-21st-century-superpower/ (Accessed: 8 February 2021).

194. Guest blogger for net politics. (2015) *India's Internet Diplomacy: Reading the Tea Leaves.* Available at: https://www.cfr.org/blog/indias-internet-diplomacy-reading-tea-leaves (Accessed: 4 December 2021).

195. Jones, A. (2007) *China's Rise and American Hegemony: Towards a Peaceful Co-Existence*. Available at: https://www.e-ir.info/2007/12/22/chinas-rise-and-american-hegemony-towards-a-peaceful-co-existence/, (Accessed: 16 December 2021).

196. Gupta, K. (2019) *India's soft power: empowering people to share their 'Incredible Indian' story.* Available at: https://www.kcl.ac.uk/news/india-soft-power-empowering-people-share-incredible-indian-story (Accessed: 19 November 2020)

197. Held, D. (2021) *Why China Should Re-Strategize its' Wolf Warrior Diplomacy.* Available at: https://www.e-ir.info/2021/01/12/why-china-should-re-strategize-its-wolf-warrior-diplomacy/ (Accessed: 21 February 2022).

198. Herrington. (2011) *Why the Rise of China Will Not Lead to Global Hegemony*. Available at: https://www.e-ir.info/2011/07/15/why-the-precarious-rise-of-china-will-not-lead-to-global-hegemony/ (Accessed: 15 December 2021).

199. Iwanek, K. (2021) *Restoring Ties by Restoring Monuments: Indian Diplomacy in Southeast Asia*, Available at: https://thediplomat.com/2021/02/restoring-ties-by-restoring-monuments-indian-diplomacy-in-southeast-asia/, (Accessed: 17 October 2021)

200. Jaishankar, D. (2018) *India rising: Soft power and the world's largest democracy*. Available at: https://www.brookings.edu/opinions/india-rising-soft-power-and-the-worlds-largest-democracy/ (Accessed: 19 September 2020).

201. Jha, A.N. (2021) *An opportunity for Digital India*. Available at: https://indianexpress.com/article/opinion/columns/made-in-india-digital-diplomacy-7695385/ (Accessed: 4 January 2022).

202. Jha, P.S. (2021) *What Lies Behind China's Belt and Road Initiative*? Available at: https://thewire.in/world/china-belt-and-road-initiative-trade (Accessed: 16 January 2022).

203. Joshi, N. (2021) *Digital Diplomacy: AI As A Tool To Strengthen International Relations.* Available at: https://www.forbes.com/sites/naveenjoshi/2021/12/12/digital-diplomacy-ai-as-a-tool-to-strengthen-international-relations/?sh=2930c4986983 (Accessed: 2 February 2022).

204. Karthik, R. (2020) *Management is India's most successful soft power*. Available at: https://www.theweek.in/theweek/specials/2020/12/10/management-is-india-most-successful-soft-power.html (Accessed: 2 February 2022)

205. Kaul, A. (2021) *Explained: PM Modi's Role In Promoting India's Culture As Soft Power And Revival Of Holy Shrines*. Available at: https://www.republicworld.com/india-news/general-news/pm-modis-role-in-promoting-indias-culture-as-soft-power-and-revival-of-holy-shrines.html (Accessed: 2 January 2022).

206. Kawakita, K. (2020) *Are We Entering an "Asian Century: The Possibility of a New International Order*. Available at: https://www.e-ir.info/2020/07/04/are-we-entering-an-asian-century-the-possibility-of-a-new-international-order/ (Accessed: 18 December 2021).

207. Kheng. K.S, Reddy. S (2022) *India, Covid-19 and the Global Health Agenda*. Available at: https://www.orfonline.org/expert-speak/india-covid-19-and-the-global-health-agenda/ (Accessed: 26 February 2022)

208. Kulkarni. (2021) *Azadi ka Amrit Mahotsav and Cultural Diplomacy*. Available at: https://diplomatist.com/2021/10/14/azadi-ka-amrit-mahotsav-and-cultural-diplomacy/ (Accessed: 24 December 2021).

209. Kim. (2015) *The Fundamental Dynamics of East Asia Security by PRC Maritime Expansion*.Available at: https://www.e-ir.info/2015/10/19/the-fundamental-dynamics-of-east-asia-security-by-prc-maritime-expansion/ (Accessed: 5 August 2021).

210. Kumar, Y. (2020) *Opinion - 'Soft power, pillar of Indian foreign policy.* Available at: https://www.aa.com.tr/en/analysis/opinion-soft-power-pillar-of-indian-foreign-policy/1942745 (Accessed: 24 October 2021).

211. Lekakis. N (2019) *The Limits of Soft Power-Sports Diplomacy Templates in IR Research*. Available at: https://www.e-ir.info/2019/06/23/the-limits-of-soft-power-sports-diplomacy-templates-in-ir-research/ (Accessed: 23 October 2020).

212. Live Mint. (2018) *India's soft power push: just following a fad*. Available at: https://www.livemint.com/Opinion/JU8gsI713CuUuvMgD8GUrM/Indias-soft-power-push-just-following-a-fad.html (Accessed: 30 November 2019)

213. Livemint. (2017) *The role of states in foreign policy.* Available at: https://www.livemint.com/Opinion/pWTDtrHhs9TyrVQKHb29gJ/The-role-of-states-in-foreign-policy.html (Accessed: 6 December 2021).

214. Mahapatra, C. (2021) *Indian foreign policy: Looking back and then forward*. Available at: https://www.firstpost.com/india/2021-indian-foreign-policy-looking-back-and-then-forward-10246321.html (Accessed: 14 January 2022).

215. Manallack, S. (2021) *With Rise of China and India, West Has to Learn the Asian Way of Diplomacy in 2022*. Available at: https://www.news18.com/news/opinion/with-rise-of-china-india-west-has-to-learn-asian-way-of-diplomacy-in-2022-4584683.html (Accessed: 15 January 2022).

216. McCarthy, T. (2011) *Assessing China and India's New Role in Africa*. Available at: https://www.e-ir.info/2011/07/26/assessing-china-and-india%e2%80%99s-new-role-in-africa/ (Accessed: 2 November 2020).

217. Medcalf, R. (2011) *India's New World: Civil Society in the Making of Foreign Policy*. Available at: https://apo.org.au/sites/default/files/resource-files/2011-05/apo-nid24707.pdf. (Accessed 4 October 2020)

218. Mcclory. J (2019) *Until 2016, India was on course to break into soft power group of 30 nations. Then it fell*. Available at: https://theprint.in/opinion/until-2016-india-was-on-course-to-break-into-soft-power-group-of-30-nations-then-it-fell/221298/, (Accessed: 21 November 2019).

219. Nanda, P. (2014) *Good Governance and Foreign Policy.* Available at: http://www.indiandefencereview.com/good-governance-and-foreign-policy/ (Accessed: 5 October, 2020)

220. Nath, D. (2020) *Importance of soft power is increasing globally: ICCR chief Vinay Sahasrabuddhe*. Available at: https://www.thehindu.com/news/national/importance-of-soft-power-is-increasing-globally-iccr-chief-vinay-sahasrabuddhe/article31292723.ece (Accessed: 14 October 2020)

221. Nayar, M. (2021) *Modi has been working to turn India's Buddhist heritage into strategic asset* Available at: https://www.theweek.in/theweek/cover/2021/09/16/modi-has-been-working-to-turn-india-buddhist-heritage-into-strategic-asset.html (Accessed: 4 December 2021)

222. Nayar, N. (2021) *Para diplomacy in Northeast India: Assam Acts East*. Available at: https://csep.org/blog/paradiplomacy-in-northeast-india-assam-acts-east/ (Accessed: 9 December 2021)

223. Nayar, M. (2021) *Modi has been working to turn India's Buddhist heritage into strategic asset*. Available at:https://www.theweek.in/theweek/cover/2021/09/16/modi-has-been-working-to-turn-india-buddhist-heritage-into-strategic-asset.html (Accessed: 27 January 2022)

224. Norman, K. E. (2013) *Definitions, Ideas, Visions and Challenges for Cultural Diplomacy*. Available at: https://www.e-ir.info/2013/01/03/definitions-ideas-visions-and-challenges-for-cultural-diplomacy/ (Accessed: 9 March 2021).

225. Majumder, A. (2020) *Modi's disease diplomacy shows India's growing soft power, as he shapes global coalition against coronavirus*. Available at: https://www.rt.com/op-ed/483340-modi-india-coronavirus-epidemic/ (Accessed: 19 December 2020).

226. Martin, P. (2015) *Yoga Diplomacy: Narendra Modi's Soft Power Strategy*", https://www.foreignaffairs.com/articles/india/2015-01-25/yoga-diplomacy, (Accessed: 22 April 2022).

227. Mishra, M. K (2016) *The Impacts and Limits of India's Soft Power*. Available at https://www.georgetownjournalofinternationalaffairs.org/online-edition/the-impacts-and-limits-of-indias-soft-power (Accessed: 25 November 2019)

228. Mohan, R. (2014) *Modi's Diplomacy: Yoga, Democracy, and India's Soft Power*.Available at: https://carnegieindia.org/2014/12/15/modi-s-diplomacy-yoga-democracy-and-india-s-soft-power-pub-57521 (Accessed: 18 September 2019)

229. Mukherjee, B. (2019) *India's culture Diplomacy and Soft Power*. Available at: https://www.mea.gov.in/distinguished-lectures-detail.htm?855 (Accessed: 29 October 2019).

230. Mustafa. (2013) *Doordarshan diplomacy*. Available at: https://www.gatewayhouse.in/doordarshan-diplomacy/ (Accessed: 3 March 2022).

231. Nelles. M. (2012) *China's Growing Cyber War Capacities*. Available at: https://www.e-ir.info/2012/07/29/chinas-growing-cyber-war-capacities/ (Accessed: 8 April 2022).

232. Pant, H.V.(2022) *India's Soft-Power Strategy*. Available at: https://www.outlookindia.com/website/story/indias-soft-power-strategy/295206, (Accessed: 24 March 2022).

233. Pant. H.V, Singh. N. (2020) *Indian Foreign Policy and Its Aspirations: Institutional Design Matters*. Available at: https://www.orfonline.org/expert-speak/indian-foreign-policy-and-its-aspirations/ (Accessed: 28 January 2022).

234. Parthasarathy, G. (2021) *The vaccine can be India's soft power.* Available at: https://www.thehindubusinessline.com/opinion/columns/g-parthasarathy/the-vaccine-can-be-indias-soft-power/article33551725.ece (Accessed: 23 January 2022)

235. Pathak, S. (2015) *The "Peace" in China's Peaceful Rise*. Available at: https://www.e-ir.info/2015/10/15/the-peace-in-chinas-peaceful-rise/ (Accessed: 24 January 2022).

236. Peri. D. (2021) *India far ahead of China in leading the world with ideas: Rajnath Singh*. Available at: https://www.thehindu.com/news/national/unprovoked-aggression-at-himalayan-frontiers-reminder-of-how-world-is-changing-rajnath-singh-at-ficci-annual-general-meeting/article61938599.ece (Accessed: 29 January 2022)

237. Petrovsky, V. (1998), *Diplomacy as an instrument of good governance*. Available on: https://www.diplomacy.edu/resource/diplomacy-as-an-instrument-of-good-governance/ (Accessed 8 November 2019).

238. Pillalamarri, A. (2016) *5 Ways India Can Become a Soft Power Superpower*. Available at: https://thediplomat.com/2016/07/5-ways-india-can-become-a-soft-power-superpower/ (Accessed: 23 September 2019)

239. Prakash, A. (2021). *What India needs to address to achieve 'great power' status*. Available at: https://www.deccanherald.com/specials/sunday-spotlight/what-india-needs-to-address-to-achieve-great-power-status-1064748.html (Accessed: 4 January 2022)

240. Prakash, I. (2021), *The Growth of Soft Power in the World's Largest Democracy,* Available at: https://moderndiplomacy.eu/2021/01/19/the-growth-of-soft-power-in-the-worlds-largest-democracy/ (Accessed: 22 August 2021).

241. Prasenjit, P. (2021) *India Independence: Diaspora power - From remittances to diplomacy, overseas Indians script India's success story.* Available at: https:/

/www.wionews.com/india-news/india-independence-diaspora-power-from-remittances-to-diplomacy-overseas-indians-script-indias-success-story-405316 (Accessed: 10 December 2021)

242. Pratap, B. (2015) *India's Cultural Diplomacy: Present Dynamics, Challenges And Future Prospects.* Available at: https://www.semanticscholar.org/paper/India%27s-Cultural-Diplomacy%3A-Present-Dynamics%2C-And-Pratap/2f0c6f9e1d8800b277ba1559c76fbff0b6552d48 (Accessed: 23 September 2021)

243. PTI. (2017) *Indian culture has soft power to make it influential leader: Shashi Tharoor*. Available at https://economictimes.indiatimes.com/news/politics-and-nation/indian-culture-has-soft-power-to-make-it-influentialleader-shashi-tharoor/articleshow/59065514.cms, (Accessed: 9 November 2019)

244. PTI. (2020) *India's Culture, Art Integral To Its Soft Power: Foreign Secretary*. Available at: https://www.ndtv.com/india-news/indias-culture-art-integral-to-its-soft-power-foreign-secretary-harsh-vardhan-shringla-2334943 (Accessed: 5 March 2021)

245. Purayil. M.P, Gujjeti. A (2021) *What the Second Wave of COVID-19 Means for India's Public Diplomacy*. Available at: https://thediplomat.com/2021/04/what-the-second-wave-of-covid-19-means-for-indias-public-diplomacy/ (Accessed: 5 October 2021).

246. Quinn, A. (2018) *How History Shapes India's Foreign Policy Goals*. Available at: https://www.e-ir.info/2018/08/04/how-history-shapes-indias-foreign-policy-goals/ (Accessed: 2 March 2020).

247. Rajagopalan, R. (2021) *A rather thin Foreign Policy debate*. Available at: https://www.orfonline.org/expert-speak/a-rather-thin-foreign-policy-debate/, (Accessed: 12 November 2021)

248. Ramachandran, S. (2015) *India's Soft Power Potential*. Available at: https://thediplomat.com/2015/05/indias-soft-power-potential/, (Accessed: 4 December 2021)

249. Ramachandran, S. (2013) *The Indian Foreign Service: Worthy of an Emerging Power?* Available at: https://thediplomat.com/2013/07/the-indian-foreign-service-worthy-of-an-emerging-power/ (Accessed: 19 November 2020).

250. Rana, K. (2013) *Re-setting India's public diplomacy*. Available at: https://www.business-standard.com/article/opinion/kishan-s-rana-re-setting-india-s-public-diplomacy-111011600021_1.html (Accessed: 24 October 2020).

251. Rana, K. S. (2013*) Re-setting India's public diplomacy*. Available at: https://www.business-standard.com/article/opinion/kishan-s-rana-re-setting-india-s-public-diplomacy-111011600021_1.html (Accessed: 10 November 2019).

252. Rao, N. (2021) *Editorial: On the wane*. Available at: https://www.telegraphindia.com/opinion/india-must-reconnect-with-its-core-strengths/cid/1845248 (Accessed: 27 January 2022)

253. Rao, N. (2021) *India's soft power credentials vs China lie in open society, diversity* Available at: https://timesofindia.indiatimes.com/india/indias-soft-power-credentials-vs-china-lie-in-open-society-diversity-nirupama-rao/articleshow/88510188.cms (Accessed: 29 January 2022)

254. Roy, A. G (2020) *Opinion – Virtual Diplomacy in India.* Available at: https://www.e-ir.info/2020/06/11/opinion-virtual-diplomacy-in-india/ (Accessed: 23 October 2020).

255. Roche, E. (2021) *Foreign ministry to promote yoga for well being in show of soft power*. Available at: https://www.livemint.com/news/foreign-ministry-asks-to-embrace-yoga-to-battle-after-effects-of-covid-11624178206377.html (Accessed: 19 December 2022).

256. Roy, A. (2017) *Raj Kapoor and India's Foremost Cinematic Soft Power Breakthrough.* Available at: https://www.e-ir.info/2017/01/23/raj-kapoor-and-indias-foremost-cinematic-soft-power-breakthrough/ (Accessed: 11 November 2019).

257. Roy, A. (2020) *The Trouble With India's Soft Power Apparatus*. Available at: https://thediplomat.com/2020/02/the-trouble-with-indias-soft-power-apparatus/ (Accessed: 14 March 2020).

258. Roy. J, Das. N and S. Shreya. (2021) *India must use SDG framework to strengthen developmental diplomacy*. Available at: https://www.orfonline.org/expert-speak/india-must-use-sdg-framework-strengthen-developmental-diplomacy/ (Accessed: 17 October 2021)

259. Sahasrabuddhe, V. (2021*) India has started to assert its soft power.* Available at: https://www.newindianexpress.com/opinions/columns/2021/nov/10/india-has-started-to-assert-its-soft-power-2381569.html (Accessed: 28 January 2022).

260. Saran, S. (2020) *India's diplomatic space may shrink as govt picks hardline political agenda*. Available at https://www.business-standard.com/article/economy-policy/india-s-diplomatic-space-may-shrink-as-govt-picks-hardline-political-agenda-120010200436_1.html (Accessed: 18 April 2022)

261. Sareen, S. (2018) *When soft power is not enough.* Available at: https://www.orfonline.org/research/when-soft-power-not-enough-44889/ (Accessed: 20 November 2019)

262. Sarmah. S.P (2021) *Paradiplomacy: The possibilities, and challenges, of Assam-Bangladesh relations*. Available at: https://www.hindustantimes.com/opinion/paradiplomacy-the-possibilities-and-challenges-of-assam-bangladesh-relations-101624019605196.html (Accessed: 30 November 2021)

263. Sawant, M. (2020) *Opinion – The Civilization Narrative: China's Grand Strategy to Rule the World*. Available at: https://www.e-ir.info/2020/05/10/opinion-the-civilisation-narrative-chinas-grand-strategy-to-rule-the-world/ (Accessed: 13 January 2022).

264. Sengupta. H (2018), *Can Indian soft power reinvent itself?*. Available at: https://www.fortuneindia.com/opinion/can-indian-soft-power-reinvent-itself/102734 (Accessed: 3 October 2020)

265. Sengupta, J. (2017) *India's cultural and civilizational influence on Southeast Asia*, . Available at: https://www.orfonline.org/expert-speak/indias-cultural-and-civilizational-influence-on-southeast-asia/ (Accessed: 8 November 2020)

266. Shahi, D. (2016) *Teaching International Relations in India: From Pedagogy to Andragogy*. Available at: https://www.e-ir.info/2016/10/29/teaching-international-relations-in-india-from-pedagogy-to-andragogy/ (Accessed: 5 June 2020)

267. Shankar, R. (2021) *The evil empire: Is China on its way to world domination*?".Available at: https://www.newindianexpress.com/magazine/2021/jun/06/the-evil-empire-is-china-on-its-way-to-world-domination-2311359.html (Accessed: 8 October 2021)

268. Sibal, S. (2021) *Indian govt's ICCR working to spread 'spirituality as soft power.* Available at: https://zeenews.india.com/india/indian-govts-iccr-working-to-spread-spirituality-as-soft-power-2410139.html (Accessed: 29 January 2022)

269. Sidhu, G.K. (2021) *Smokes and media": Public Diplomacy in India-Pakistan.* Available at: https://diplomatist.com/2021/04/29/smokes-and-media-public-diplomacy-in-india-pakistan/ (Accessed: 3 November 2021).

270. Sitharaman, S. (2013) *Chinese Grand Strategy and the Exacerbation of the Sino-Indian Territorial Dispute*. Available at: https://www.e-ir.info/2013/08/21/chinese-grand-strategy-and-the-exacerbation-of-the-sino-indian-territorial-dispute/ (Accessed: 18 April 2019).

271. Sekhar, P. (2021) *India is a soft superpower with a smart and secured governance strategy*. Available at https://www.neweurope.eu/article/india-is-a-soft-superpower-with-a-smart-and-secured-governance-strategy/ (Accessed: 21 January 2022)

272. Sreenivasan, T.P. (2015) *Foreign Service must remain elitist.* Available at: https://www.thehindu.com/opinion/op-ed/foreign-service-must-remain-elitist/article7350788.ece/amp/ (Accessed: 23 November 2019).

273. Srinivas, S. (2021), *The 2022 Winter Olympics: A cold reception?*. Available at: https://www.orfonline.org/expert-speak/2022-winter-olympics/, (Accessed: 28 January 2022).

274. Stobdan, P. (2020) *Soft power can be effective.* Available at: https://indianexpress.com/article/opinion/india-china-galwan-faceoff-soft-power-can-be-effective-6499695/ (Accessed: 25 October 2020).

275. Thapar, K. (2021) *The roots of the India-China discord.* Available at: https://www.hindustantimes.com/opinion/the-roots-of-the-india-china-discord-101624115010255.html (Accessed: 6 September 2021).

276. Tharoor, S. (2021) *India must remain safe for diversity*. Available at: https://www.thehindu.com/opinion/op-ed/india-must-remain-safe-for-diversity/article37406310.ece (Accessed: 28 November 2021).

277. Tourangham, M. (2020) *India's Rise and Why Soft Power Matters.* Available at https://diplomatist.com/2020/08/25/indias-rise-and-why-soft-power-matters/, (Accessed: 29 October 2020)

278. TPT Bureau. (2021) *India the Global Soft Superpower with Smart & Secured Governance Strategy*. Available at: https://thepolicytimes.com/india-the-global-soft-superpower-with-smart-secured-governance-strategy/ (Accessed: 19 January 2022).

279. Uddin, Z. (2018) *Soft and Normative Power: The Power of Attraction in International Politics*. Available at: https://www.e-ir.info/2011/10/01/soft-and-normative-power-the-power-of-attraction-in-international-politics/ (Accessed: 3 December 2019).

280. Varisco, A. E. (2013) *Towards a Multi-Polar International System: Which Prospects for Global Peace.* Available at: https://www.e-ir.info/2013/06/03/

towards-a-multi-polar-international-system-which-prospects-for-global-peace/ (Accessed: 19 October 2020).

281. Varma, P. (2021) *Why soft power matters: It's an invaluable asset. India must not diminish its stock by weakening its democracy*, Available at: https://timesofindia.indiatimes.com/blogs/toi-edit-page/why-soft-power-matters-its-an-invaluable-asset-india-must-not-diminish-its-stock-by-weakening-its-democracy/ (Accessed: 27 January 2022).

282. Villanueva, R. (2014) *Contradictions Implicit in the Idea of Global Civil Society*. Available at: https://www.e-ir.info/2014/07/02/contradictions-implicit-in-the-idea-of-global-civil-society/ (Accessed: 8 December 2022).

283. Welsh, T. (2020) *Mexico releases Latin America's first feminist foreign policy*. Available at: https://www.devex.com/news/mexico-releases-latin-america-s-first-feminist-foreign-policy-96363 (Accessed: 10 December 2021).

284. Wilson, A. (2021) *How Narendra Modi Nearly Lost His Way in 2021. Available at:* https://foreignpolicy.com/2021/12/24/modi-india-farmer-protests-covid-kashmir/ (Accessed: 29 January 2022)

285. Yadav, P. (2021) *India's real soft power is commitment to democracy, and 'andolanjeevis' are integral to it*. Available at: https://theprint.in/campus-voice/indias-real-soft-power-is-commitment-to-democracy-and-andolanjeevis-are-integral-to-it/610552/ (Accessed: 23 December 2021).

286. Younus, U. (2019) *India's Foreign Policy Evolution*. Available at: https://thediplomat.com/2019/03/indias-foreign-policy-evolution/ (Accessed: 6 October 2019).

287. Yunus, A. (2018) *One Belt, One Road': Sign of a Revisionist or Integrative China*. Available at: https://www.e-ir.info/2018/07/22/one-belt-one-road-sign-of-a-revisionist-or-integrative-china/ (Accessed: 17 January 2022).